Responsive Classroom

MW00611590

Strengthening
the
Parent-Teacher
Partnership

Jane Cofie

ISBN: 978-1-950317-17-2
Library of Congress Control Number: 2021946438

Center for Responsive Schools, Inc.
85 Avenue A, P.O. Box 718
Turners Falls, MA 01376-0718

800-360-6332
www.crslearn.org

Third printing 2023

Contents

ACKNOWLEDGMENTS

Many people encouraged me and helped me grow in numerous ways in the writing of this book. In addition to all my experiences as an educator and as a parent, several parents and educators willingly shared their thoughts, stories, tips, and ideas with me. Their input was invaluable and helped enhance the work of this book. Among these educators and parents are: Talisha Alexander, Cate Avery-Jagla, Michelle Benson, Christine Diaz, Nicole Doner, Raine Hackler, Golda Hector, Kirsten Howard, Faye Jennings, Rozi Khakpour, Dr. Maureen Marshall, Nikki Odugbose, Shala Ott, Karen Poplawski, Charles Quartey, Ann Rose Santoro, and Suzanne Wright.

A special thank you to three key encouragers and supporters throughout the writing of this book. Donnett Vicente, a parent of three and a very dear friend, readily shared many of her experiences as a parent volunteer at her children's schools in the United States and overseas and offered many hours in helping me process and think through some of the content in this book. Parent-teacher conversations with Jen Berndsen continually elevated and boosted my thinking. Dr. Joe Tilley not only read the manuscript but also offered words of encouragement and wisdom along the way, reminding me that "your unique perspective on something may just be the difference in someone's understanding."

Thank you to my sisters and faithful cheerleaders, Harriet, Josey, Jeraldine, and Joann. Their knowledge and expertise as educators and as parents has always inspired me to continually reflect on and refine what I do and to strive for what is best for children as an educator and as a parent.

My parents, Joseph and the late Thelma Cofie, not only supported and advocated for me at all times as my parents, but also served as models for me as I started my own parenting journey.

This book would not be possible without the incredible guidance, editorial skills, and wisdom of those who helped make this book a reality. Emily Hemingway's thought-provoking feedback helped me to stretch my thinking and consider multiple perspectives. Elizabeth Greene's vision for design is awe inspiring, and her creativity added colorful layers to the pages of the book. Cathy Hess's incredibly keen eye and attention to detail provided greater clarity to my thoughts. Barbara Findlen's words of wisdom, guidance, support, and feedback strengthened my writing, continually helped me to focus my thoughts, and encouraged me to keep writing.

Finally, my daughter, Sierra Rose. Her very existence enhanced my understanding of so many things, especially the power in establishing positive parent-teacher partnerships. Thank you for consciously (and sometimes unconsciously) adding to the depth of this book and being a continuous reminder to me to teach and parent with patience, compassion, empathy, and grace.

Welcome to the Partnership!

"Have a good evening, families! This concludes our back-to-school night. We would like to thank you for coming out tonight. I know we are all looking forward to a great year of learning. Safe travels home."

The principal's message over the intercom filled the room as I stood at my classroom door, saying good night to parents as they exited the room. Mr. and Mrs. S were the last to leave my classroom. They commented on the content shared and revealed they had just moved to the area and were eager to learn more about the school and how they could help.

"Let me know if you need anything. I'm happy to help out in any way I can," Mrs. S said as they departed.

It was not my first year of teaching, but it was my first year at a new school. I had a supportive grade-level teammate, and I felt comfortable with the curriculum for the year. I was getting to know the students and staff, but as the year got under way I was still navigating one piece: how to best partner with the parents of my students. I had connected with most of the parents at back-to-school night and spoken to several parents on the phone, but I knew I would need to do more in order to really get to know the parents well and for them to get to know me. Then I remembered the thoughtful invitation that Mrs. S had extended. I had a few ideas in mind, so I reached out to invite her involvement. She was thrilled to help, and we spent some time on the phone sharing ideas about specific tasks she could do to support our work in the classroom.

With each week in the classroom, Mrs. S learned more about how I supported student learning, and I learned more about her and her hopes for her child. At the same time, I was learning how to connect with and involve other parents. The strong relationship I built with Mrs. S helped me see the power in building positive relationships with parents and encouraged me to continually seek out opportunities to welcome, include, and partner with parents every year.

The Goal

The relationship between teachers and parents is an essential component in student success. Students experience greater success in school when the adults who care for them and help them learn and grow have a collaborative relationship that allows them to welcome and value one another's questions, ideas, and thoughts. Each new school year brings rich opportunities for growth: improving the delivery of the content we teach; gaining a deeper understanding of the developmental, social, academic, and emotional needs of our students; and strengthening relationships with parents that help to support student growth and success. Relationships take work. Strong relationships include communication, trust, and respect. A strong and successful partnership between educators and parents is no different.

As an educator and the parent of a middle school student, I am aware that there are a variety of views and feelings about partnering with parents. Unfortunately, some views are discouraging—there are both educators and parents who have had negative experiences and may feel that the two groups are like players on opposing teams. That mindset can negatively influence communication and hinder the journey toward a productive partnership.

But working to understand these negative experiences can go a long way toward helping us shift our attitudes, forge strong relationships, and become genuine partners to bolster student success. The impact of a strong school-home relationship on student success is so strong that this work is well worth it. We all have the ability to change our mindset to bring about lasting and positive change. We all have the ability to grow and strengthen our practices and relationships with parents. Ultimately, that is the goal. Within the pages of this book are strategies and ideas to support you in your pursuit of that goal, including relevant stories about real-life connections. My experiences as a teacher and parent, as well as research from the field and experiences of other educators, form the basis of the advice and strategies shared here. My hope is that this book provides a strong and helpful foundation for partnering well with parents.

About This Book

The purpose of this book is to encourage, strengthen, and empower educators in creating a collaborative environment that genuinely invites parents in, and to provide strategies that support educators in effectively communicating and positively collaborating with parents. Each chapter focuses on a different topic that supports the parent-teacher partnership and provides thoughts to ponder, quick tips, and practical strategies. The chapters can be read sequentially, or selected based on a particular need or area of interest.

About the Term "Parent"

Children come from homes with a variety of family structures. There are many adults who care for, guide, and nurture children through the various stages of their lives. These caring adults can be mothers, fathers, grandparents, siblings, aunts, uncles, foster parents, stepparents, and other guardians. All of these individuals are to be honored for the attention, time, and care they give to raising and guiding children. It's difficult to find one word that encompasses all these caregivers. Throughout this book, for ease of reading, I use the word "parent" to refer to any adult who is or acts as a child's caregiver, caring for, guiding, and nurturing the child's growth and learning.

As both a parent and an educator, I am constantly growing and learning. There are aspects of teaching and parenting in which I have grown significantly and other aspects I am learning to navigate. In the writing of this book, I have grown through reading, researching, and connecting with many educators and parents. You might find you are in a similar place of growth, looking to strengthen and refine, develop and learn, confirm and validate. If this describes you in any way, welcome!

"People smile.

People know my name.

They listen."

– Kirsten and Orin, parents of a
5-year-old and an 8-year-old

CHAPTER 1

A Place Where Every Parent Is Welcome

How can we create an environment in which all parents feel welcome?

My daughter's teacher smiled as she welcomed families up the ramp to the fourth grade classroom. As we entered the room, she invited students and families to sit wherever they wanted and directed students to put their supplies at a table or desk of their choice. Then she guided students to visit the classroom library to select two or three books to put in their new fourth grade book bins.

As I settled into the spot my daughter selected, I watched students eagerly explore the classroom library as the teacher seamlessly moved between greeting families at the door and connecting with parents and students in the room. I watched my daughter giggle and smile as she reconnected with friends. I watched families find places to sit and store supplies. I watched as some parents walked up to the teacher and introduced themselves and pointed out their child while other parents, like me, sat silently, taking everything in. Eventually, the teacher made her way over to me, smiled and introduced herself, then asked about my child. She shared an encouraging observation about my daughter and then handed me the packet of information she was going to review with parents shortly. I felt at ease and eagerly thumbed through the packet and watched as the teacher connected with every single parent in the room.

At some point in our lives, most of us have experienced the feeling of being in a welcoming environment—one in which we feel seen and received with pleasure. That is how we want parents to feel when they enter our schools and classrooms, gladly seen and received with pleasure. So how can we create an environment in which all parents feel welcome?

The Welcome Begins Before the Start

Parents and students alike are eager and sometimes anxious about the start of a new school year. A new school year brings different and unfamiliar experiences and, in most cases, a new teacher or two. Though parents are genuinely interested in knowing what their children will learn, they also want to know that they, and their children, will be cared for and supported. Genuinely supporting and caring for students means we need to understand their parents and create an environment in which parents feel welcome. This means taking the time to assess our beliefs about parents.

What do we believe about parents? In order to answer this question thoughtfully, we must consider a few more far-reaching questions:

- What do we believe about the role of parents in their children's education?

- What beliefs and expectations about parents have we created in our minds?

- How do we respond to parents whose backgrounds, cultures, experiences, and beliefs are different from our own?

- How do we respond to family structures or configurations that are unfamiliar or unique?

- How do we respond to different parenting styles and values?

- How do we speak about parents during meetings, in the hallways, at lunch, in the front office, and with colleagues?

- How do our perceptions of parents shift after challenging interactions or experiences?

These questions, as well as many others, may require some additional exploration in order to bring deeper thoughts to the forefront. This process of exploration is important because our beliefs and actions are influenced by our experiences. Some of our experiences are consciously stored in our minds while some experiences are unconsciously stored (Dee and Gershenson 2017). Whether or not we are conscious of them, these experiences influence our actions and beliefs. Asking ourselves probing questions such as these helps us get to the heart of our beliefs about parents. Assessing our beliefs allows us to bring to light any unconscious biases that might be getting in the way of creating a welcoming environment for all parents, and work toward addressing and minimizing those biases, in turn enabling us to connect with parents in a positive way when we meet them.

The First Encounter

Several years ago, I started presenting professional development workshops for elementary educators. When I first started, during my training, my instructor spent a good amount of time helping us understand the importance of the initial introduction—the first encounter. The first encounter is the opening section of the workshop in which we greet all the workshop participants, tell a little bit about ourselves, and set the tone for the day. I always shared my name, where I was from, my number of years in the field of education, the grade levels I had taught, and a little about my daughter. My goal was to share an adequate amount of background information so that participants could get to know a little about me but not so much as to lose the participants' attention or feel like I was rambling. I managed to keep my introduction to a few concise sentences. Though I was pleased with the brevity of my personal introduction, the purpose of the first encounter is not to create a concise introduction. That is just part of it. The true purpose is to set the tone by creating a welcoming climate of safety and trust.

The same is true when we consider the type of climate we want to create with parents. When I think back to some of my early first encounters with parents, I'm not sure that I understood their purpose, as I was immersed with setting up my classroom and checking items off of my "Before the Start of the School Year" to-do list. During my first couple of years of teaching, I remember being very nervous. Of course, I wanted to make a good first impression. Who doesn't? I wanted to make sure that everything was perfect before families came to my classroom for the first time. I wanted everything to be beautifully organized and appear as though I had everything under control. There is certainly nothing wrong with being organized and composed. However, it is important not to lose sight of the true focus: establishing a welcoming climate that sets the tone for establishing meaningful connections with students and families.

Whether schools host a back-to-school night, an open house, home visits, or another beginning-of-the-year tradition, we want our focus to be creating an environment in which parents feel welcome, seen, and heard. When parents feel seen and heard from the start, they are more likely to feel that we have the same goal in mind: doing what is best for their child to ensure success. Simply telling parents we have the same goal is not as effective as showing them, from our first encounter, that their child's safety and success are our priorities.

Start with an informal connection. Initially connecting with parents in an informal way such as a school picnic, barbeque, parent coffee, or ice cream social allows for a more relaxed feeling for both parents and teachers. An informal event can even be something more low-key, like inviting families to drop off or pick up supplies and materials during the hours in which you will be in the classroom setting up. At an informal event or gathering, there's no pressure to share curriculum or class schedules. This is not an occasion for a formal presentation but more of a time for parents and teachers to get to know one another.

Make welcoming parents an important part of formal gatherings and meetings. There is likely a program or schedule to follow when it comes to hosting formal school events for families. If an event takes place in individual classrooms, take time to greet parents at the classroom door and make personal connections before getting into the subject matter of the event. In the case of a schoolwide event that does not lend itself easily to greeting parents at the door, consider mingling and connecting with as many parents as possible before the event begins.

Keep the Welcome Going

Creating a welcoming environment for parents extends beyond the first encounter and beginning-of-the-year events and activities. In order for parents to feel truly accepted and heard, we have to keep welcoming them back throughout the school year with quality communication and by creating ways to continually strengthen positive relationships with them.

It took me a few years of teaching to really understand the importance of consistent and meaningful communication with parents. The more effective the communication, the stronger the relationship (Comer and Haynes 1991; Epstein 1986; Hoover-Dempsey and Walker 2002). I communicated with parents in various ways, from meetings to phone calls to newsletters sent home every two weeks. I was consistent about sharing general information like upcoming units of study, field trips, school events, learning strategies, and ways to support at home. All of the communication I sent home to parents invited them to reach out if they had any questions or concerns. The content of my communication was useful and important. However, most of my communication was for the purpose of conveying impersonal information. It was often broad or general and not specific to the parent or student. Just as it is important to make sure that every student is known and significant in our classrooms, we want to create that same feeling for parents when we communicate with them.

Most likely, parents know that we know our content or the curriculum well. They also want to know that we know their child well and that we are open to the knowledge that they have about their child. When our forms of communication are more personal and specific, parents feel more at ease and welcome to share their thoughts and concerns. When I connected with parents more frequently through more specific and personal types of communication, my relationships with these parents evolved and became stronger. For example, I emailed the parents of one of my fourth grade students every week. They were concerned about her progress and we all felt that weekly updates would allow us to more quickly identify areas that needed attention. In each email exchange, they shared what they were noticing at home and I shared what I was noticing at school. I learned more about them and their hopes for their child, and they learned more about me and the ways in which I was supporting their child. They felt more valued and empowered to share their thoughts, questions, and concerns.

My understanding of the link between effective communication and relationships with parents expanded when I became a parent. I started thinking about and viewing communication through both lenses. When I felt welcome in my daughter's classroom and the communication was more personal, I felt heard and more empowered to share my thoughts and concerns. My communication with the teacher was specific and focused on following up on topics we had previously discussed. Her communication with me was similar, and she contacted me to share successes and next steps. I had a stronger understanding of how my daughter was being supported at school, and I felt comfortable sharing how I was supporting my daughter at home. The opposite was also true: When the communication I received was more general and did not extend beyond a conference at the start of the year, I felt less heard and less welcome to share my concerns and thoughts about my daughter's learning.

Maintaining a welcoming environment takes consistent attention to building and strengthening relationships with parents beyond effective communication. Similar to how we build relationships with students, we can begin by seeking answers to general questions, such as:

- What are parents' communication preferences? (Email? Text? Phone call? Home visit? Communication app?)

- Is there more availability during the day or in the evening?

- What languages are spoken at home?

- What are some of the family traditions?

- What talents and experiences are parents willing to share?

Questions like these provide a good starting point and pave the way to seeking out more opportunities to connect with parents as the school year progresses.

Many schools are eager to involve parents in daily activities, and parents, when able, appreciate being included. The classroom teacher can help build and nurture a welcoming environment that invites parents in and values them for their contributions, expertise, support, and knowledge. In a school that embraces parents, the staff also learns to acknowledge and welcome diverse perspectives (Henderson and Mapp 2002). When parents feel seen and heard, they are more likely to be involved in their child's learning, which has many significant benefits such as greater student achievement, a more positive attitude toward school, and improved student behavior (Epstein and Salinas 2004).

Quick Tips

- **Remember to smile.** Whether we see parents in the office or the cafeteria, or as they are walking down the hallway to our classrooms, a welcoming smile can go a long way. It sets the tone for the interaction as well as future interactions. Keep in mind that we want the entire school environment to be a welcoming place for parents. Thus, a welcoming smile shared with any parent—those of our current or former students, or parents we have yet to meet—sends the message that all parents are welcome.

- **Say something.** Along with a smile, a simple "Hello," "Welcome," or "Good morning" lets parents know that they are seen and significant.

- **Use names whenever possible.** Our names are strongly connected to our identities. Acknowledging someone by name sends the message that they are seen and important. Whenever possible, invite parents to share the name they would prefer to be called. For some of us, remembering names is our strong suit, and for others, it is more of a challenge. It is okay to be honest and let a parent know we have forgotten their name with a simple statement such as "I'm still working on remembering names. Please remind me of your name again." Then state their name immediately after they share it—not only to confirm the pronunciation, but also to let them know that they are heard.

- **Be mindful of cultural differences.** Shaking hands is not the norm or preference for everyone. Some people prefer not to shake hands for health, religious, or cultural reasons. People from different cultures have different ways of greeting one another, such as a bow or a kiss on the cheek. Keeping this in mind, a simple smile or gentle wave can be used to acknowledge parents while respecting various cultures and preferences.

Steps Toward Partnering: Strategies to Welcome Parents

- **Welcome/introduction letter.** Sending a brief welcome letter at the start of the year, either electronically or by mail, is a wonderful way to make an early connection with parents. A welcome letter can include a brief introduction, some details about what students will be learning that year, and contact information. Consider including QR codes or links that parents can access that will provide responses to frequently asked questions and information about upcoming events.

- **Proactive questions and answers.** The beginning of a new school year is often a time of uncertainty and questions. Taking a proactive approach to questions can help parents feel more at ease. Reach out to parents before an informal meeting or formal event to find out what questions they might have, and then determine the best way to respond. For example, it might be reasonable to call parents if there are just a few responses to provide. For a greater number of parents or questions, it might be more realistic to compile frequently asked questions and responses into a format that all parents can easily view or access like a letter, media post, or email.

- **Early connections.** Before an initial formal meeting, consider ways to connect with parents in a more informal or relaxed way. For a variety of reasons, parents may not be able to make it to a beginning-of-the-year event, but there are many ways we can accommodate busy schedules and family obligations to help parents feel welcome and included. Tried and true strategies include postcards and letters sent in the mail, emails, home visits, phone calls, texts, informal meetings, or early conferences.

- **Early virtual classroom visit and virtual meet and greet.** Technology provides additional ways to connect with parents. Consider using a digital platform or app to introduce yourself and welcome parents. Parents and students can take a virtual tour of the classroom and get to know more about the teacher. Also consider posting a welcome video that parents can view at a time that is most convenient. The posted video can include an introduction, a glimpse into the classroom, and invitations to upcoming formal events. Provide a few ways for parents to ask questions after the video through email, surveys, a comment section, video responses, or phone calls.

- **Formal or schoolwide welcoming events.** Many schools organize formal welcoming events at the start of the school year such as an open house, a back-to-school night, community visits, or a back-to-school fair. For some parents, the timing for these events works well, but for others parents it presents a challenge. When parents are not able to attend beginning-of-the-year events, it can be difficult to establish or sustain a strong connection. Consider including additional opportunities or providing different ways for parents to access back-to-school events, such as livestreaming or making a video recording for parents to view at a more convenient time.

The school environment feels like a family that supports all students."

–Michelle and Thomas, parents of children ages 12 and 17

CHAPTER 2

A Culturally Plural Classroom

How do we honor students' cultures in our classrooms?

In the sixth grade, I was given an assignment in which I had to give an oral presentation about my culture. My mother and father were both born and raised in Accra, Ghana, so most of my research consisted of having conversations with my parents about what life was like for them before they came to the United States. Most of the information my parents shared was familiar because it was seamlessly woven into the way my sisters and I were raised, from the foods we ate, to the language spoken at home, to traditions to which we had grown accustomed.

On presentation day, I felt comfortable and confident about all that I would be sharing with my classmates. After all, I had been immersed in Ghanaian culture since birth. It was familiar and I knew it well. At the close of my presentation, it was time for questions from my classmates. Nothing could have prepared me for the types of questions they asked. "Do people wear clothes?" "Where do people keep the lions?" "Do people have pet goats?" Though there were students from a variety of different cultural backgrounds in my class, the questions made it clear to me that my classmates were likely unfamiliar with cultures similar to my own. I was flustered, and after the fourth question my teacher thankfully stopped the question and answer period, but unfortunately the damage was already done. Several years later, I still remember how I felt in that moment: ashamed and different. In that moment, I wished that I had never shared what made up so much of who I was. That was when I began to feel that it was simply better to just blend in. It is not a bad thing to encourage students to share their experiences and culture. However, without first effectively establishing a learning community in which the unique variety of cultures and experiences of every student is respectfully acknowledged, accepted, and celebrated in a manner that enhances the learning, a project such as this can highlight differences in a way that makes them seem negative, stigmatizes them, or feeds stereotypes.

As humans, we naturally have questions and feel curious about perspectives and experiences that are different from our own. Our world is made up of so many different kinds of people, which means that our classrooms are made up of students from a myriad of experiences, backgrounds, and cultures, and each student's culture is made up of a mixture of many different influences. Those differences can include characteristics such as religion, socioeconomic status, race, and ethnicity that influence how students see the world around them. We can have students in our schools who are from the same neighborhood, the same age, in the same classroom, and learning the same content, but they view that content through completely different lenses based on their cultural background. The same is true about the parents of the students we teach. We know that if we want to support student success, the way we respond to the diverse cultures of the families in our schools is crucial. We want all students to feel significant and known for all their unique qualities and everything that makes them who they are.

Multiculturalism and Cultural Pluralism

There is an incredible amount of information out there about culture. Simply searching for the word *culture* online will produce over three billion results. For our purposes, let's agree that culture includes, but is not limited to, the norms, behaviors, languages, traditions, values, symbols, and ideas of a group. Many different elements make up a person's cultural background. In order to gain a deeper understanding of how culture plays a role in our schools, we need to examine two terms: multiculturalism and cultural pluralism. The term *multiculturalism* might be more familiar for many of us. According to the International Federation of Library Associations and Institutions, multiculturalism is defined as "the co-existence of diverse cultures, where culture includes racial, religious, or cultural groups and is manifested in customary behaviors, cultural assumptions and values, patterns of thinking, and communicative styles" (IFLA n.d.). In other words, it is a presence of a variety of cultures. If we consider this definition of multiculturalism, most of our schools are multicultural, since there is likely a variety of cultures present.

Now, let's examine the term *cultural pluralism*. According to the Open Education Sociology Dictionary, cultural pluralism is defined as "a mixing of different cultures in which each culture retains its own unique identity, often referred to as a 'salad bowl'" (Bell 2013). In other words, when we consider our schools and classrooms through a multicultural lens, we see that diverse cultures, experiences, and backgrounds exist, which is an important and necessary observation. When we view our classrooms through a culturally plural lens, we are taking that observation a step further. We are acknowledging that multiple views, perspectives, and understandings will exist in addition to and separate from our own, and we consciously allow for those differences so each student retains their own cultural identity rather than being asked to blend into the dominant culture. It is like noticing a garden of beautiful assorted flowers and then taking the extra step to figure out more about each type of flower in the garden and what it needs in order to grow and flourish. We want our schools and classrooms to be culturally plural environments in which each individual student is seen and is given an equal opportunity to grow and flourish. Therefore, as our schools become increasingly diverse, it is important to be aware of how culture influences the following:

- How we build relationships with our students

- How we teach our students

- How we connect and build relationships with parents

A Culturally Plural Classroom

In order to teach our students well, we have to take the time to get to know them. We have to make time to observe them, talk to them, ask them questions, and listen to their responses so we can see what they are passionate about, what makes them smile, whom they socialize with, what causes anxiety or frustration, and what excites them. I was a very quiet student who was perfectly comfortable with going unnoticed. I worked hard and did everything I could not to call attention to myself or get in trouble. However, the classes in which I excelled most were the ones in which my teachers took time to get to know me and knew how to gently and effectively push me out of my comfortable bubble so I could be even more successful. Taking time to build and strengthen relationships is vital in creating a classroom environment in which students are seen, heard, and known for who they are individually, academically, developmentally, and culturally.

A culturally plural classroom is one in which each student is able to retain their individual cultural identity and still feel a sense of belonging in the classroom community. As we learn more about our students, it can be helpful to survey the classroom environment and ask ourselves questions such as:

- How well do I know each individual student?

- With which students do I need to build a stronger relationship?

- In what ways does the classroom environment represent the students?

- How is each individual student represented in this space?

- How are students' cultures represented in this space?

- Are all cultures equally represented?

- What adjustments might need to be made so that each student can see themselves in this environment?

- How will the environment grow with the students as the year progresses?

In my visits to schools in different states, I have seen classrooms that strongly reflect the students. In those classroom communities, I felt as if I had been given a vivid picture of the students simply because of how strongly the environment represented them. Many of these classrooms included finished student work and work in progress displayed inside and outside of the classroom, or collages of student photographs that included glimpses of their families and cultures. In some areas of the classroom it was evident that students had determined what that space should look like and include. In other classrooms, teachers displayed flags or allowed students to create flags that represented the countries from which their families had emigrated. Many classrooms included libraries that showcased literature from a variety of cultures and backgrounds. When we spend time getting to know our students, we become more attentive to everything that makes each student unique. The classroom becomes a student-centered environment that reflects each individual student.

Culturally Responsive Teaching

Genuine relationships are the foundation of culturally responsive instruction (Hammond 2013). Culturally responsive instruction, also referred to as culturally relevant teaching, is an approach in taking content and making it accessible to all students in a way that they can best understand. The term culturally relevant teaching was coined by educational theorist Gloria Ladson-Billings, who defines it as a "a pedagogy that empowers students intellectually, socially, emotionally, and politically by using cultural referents to impart knowledge, skills, and attitudes" (Ladson-Billings 1994). Once we take the time to get to know our students and better understand who they are from a cultural perspective, we are more ready and able to adjust our teaching to meet the needs of all our students. When we truly embrace the diverse cultural perspectives of our students, we recognize the powerful impact of including students' cultures in all aspects of teaching and learning. Our approach to instruction goes beyond a sprinkling of cultural studies throughout the school year or celebrating cultures and diversity only during designated months. We might begin there and then work toward taking a more culturally responsive approach to teaching that uses students' cultures, background knowledge, and experiences to support students in making deeper and more meaningful connections between their learning and their lives. Culturally responsive teaching is an approach that supports the learning needs of all students. When this approach is effectively incorporated into instruction, it strengthens students' sense of identity, promotes equity, and results in stronger student engagement in the content (Burnham 2020).

In her work on culturally responsive teaching and the brain, Zaretta Hammond explains the neuroscience behind culturally responsive teaching and offers tips on how to make lessons more culturally responsive. Culturally responsive teaching has a strong influence on the brain's memory systems and information processing structures in that it focuses on oral and active ways to transfer knowledge and make meaning (Hammond 2015). Hammond points out that many students come from backgrounds that feature oral cultural traditions and therefore tend to use memory systems of the brain that convert information into useable knowledge through various memory strategies (Hammond 2015). Hammond suggests three tips to make lessons more culturally responsive:

1. **Gamify it.** Games get the brain's attention and use cultural tools that are found in oral traditions such as repetition, solving puzzles, and making connections between things that do not seem to be related.

2. **Make it social.** Organizing learning so that students rely on each other will build on diverse students' communal orientation.

3. **Storify it.** The brain is wired to remember stories and to use story structure to make sense of the world. All students learn content more effectively if they can create a coherent narrative about the topic or process presented.

Taking a culturally responsive approach to instruction allows each student to feel valued for their unique experiences, cultures, and backgrounds and allows them to make stronger connections to their learning. It starts with building authentic relationships that acknowledge and appreciate each individual student for what makes them unique—including their cultural background.

Connecting With Parents of Different Cultures

Just as we take a culturally responsive approach to our teaching, we strive to do the same in our connections with students' families. We want to build authentic relationships with parents that embrace them as valued partners in their child's learning, partners that bring a wealth of experiences, backgrounds, and cultures.

I remember attending school gatherings with my mother and observing interactions in which my mother's attempts to ask questions or gather information were dismissed or misunderstood because of her "accent." In order to connect with parents from different cultures and truly see them as partners in their child's education, we need to begin by addressing our own reservations and beliefs about parents from cultures, backgrounds, and experiences that are different from our own. We need to take time to assess our own biases or stereotypical ideas that might be hidden after years of our own experiences and cultural influences. As humans, we all have unconscious biases. No matter how open-minded we try to be about cultures or backgrounds that are different from our own, the experiences we've had, and messages and images we've been exposed to, influence how we see other people and the world around us. The first step to authentically connecting with parents is to acknowledge our own biases and pay attention to our own behaviors and responses. We need to ask ourselves questions like:

● How do I respond to parents of different cultures?

- How do I approach parents who have different traditions or customs than I have?

- How do I connect with parents for whom English is not their first or primary language?

When we notice ourselves behaving or responding in ways that demonstrate bias, we need to correct ourselves right away and do what we can to minimize a reoccurrence. Additionally, taking time to reflect on our encounters with parents will lead to deeper processing and understanding. I once had a parent ask me if his daughter would be in a class with "those" students. My class was extremely diverse with several English speakers of other languages (ESOL) students. A defensive feeling immediately came over me, and I wanted to say, "What is that supposed to mean?" or "Who do you think you are?" Instead, I paused and asked him to share more so that I could better understand his question. After that encounter, I took time to reflect and spoke to several colleagues to gain additional insight. It turned out the underlying issue was that the parent did not have a strong understanding of how the ESOL program worked and thought that if his daughter was in a class with ESOL students, she was not in a general education class. Pausing, taking a moment to ask questions, and taking time to reflect allowed for a more productive conversation and provided greater clarity and understanding.

Consulting with a colleague or friend to gain greater insight can also help us learn how to better support parents. For example, I had a colleague who asked me for advice about securing a translator for a meeting with a parent. When she first met with this parent, a translator was not present and communication was difficult. From having spent time with this family in the past, I was able to provide names and contact information for translators who had previously worked with the family. Seeking support from colleagues who have worked with the family can help provide additional information for greater clarity and understanding. This will allow for greater personal growth and give way to more authentic connections with parents, which will ultimately help us be better educators and bolster student success.

Quick Tips

- **Observe.** One day as I was walking with my nine-year-old daughter and her friends, I listened as they conversed. They were talking to one another quite fluidly but referring to themselves in the third person, with statements like "Runs into tree branch and gets smacked in the face." "Laughs at Sierra Rose, then trips." They were literally narrating what they were doing as they were doing it. As I listened, I was compelled to jump in and instruct them as to the "right" way of speaking, but as I continued to observe, I realized that this was their way of communicating with one another. When faced with an unfamiliar situation, it can be tempting to jump in and "fix" it rather than observe for greater understanding. It is important to observe our students and families so that we can be aware of different styles of communication and ways families and students interact with one another. This allows us to be more aware of the variety of norms or patterns of communication so that we can be mindful of how we interact and respond.

- **Ask and learn.** It's important to acknowledge that we will not know everything about every culture represented in our schools and classrooms. It's also important to note that individuals and families are diverse even within a cultural group, so we should not attribute characteristics of one family to another family from a similar cultural background. However, we can learn a great deal just by asking questions. Reaching out to colleagues who have a relationship with parents can increase our knowledge and help us grow. We can also consider reaching out to families; asking questions increases our understanding and awareness and lets families know that we truly value their expertise and knowledge. We can use statements and questions such as:

  - "I'm not familiar with _____. Can you tell me more about _____?"

  - "This is new for me and I would like to learn more. Would you be willing to share more about _____?"

  - "What is a resource that you would recommend that would help me learn more about _____?"

  - "Would you feel comfortable sharing about _____?"

- **Learn to pronounce names correctly.** Knowing a person's name matters, and the correct pronunciation matters even more. I always feel a gentle sense of joy and pride when someone pronounces my last name correctly. But, all too often, I hear my name pronounced as "KAW-fee" instead of "KO-fee." We may not always get the pronunciation of a name correct the first time or even the third or fourth. However, it means a lot when we ask, and then keep trying to get it right. It sends the message that this person is important and worth the time and effort.

Steps Toward Partnering: Strategies to Build a Culturally Plural Environment

- **Classroom library and resources.** The resources used to support student learning are beneficial tools for empowering students. At the start of the school year and periodically throughout the year, take an inventory of the resources and books in the classroom. Are they representative of the students? Can students "see" themselves in the literature and resources offered? Are they current? Are they easily accessible or featured only during certain times of the year? Consider the databases and online resources that students access. Do they represent a variety of backgrounds and cultures?

- **Front office and entryway.** What do people see when they enter the school building? The entryway and front office should provide a clear picture of the community of learners that resides there. When possible, the front office or entryway should include photographs of families from the school or student artwork. Additionally, the signage in these areas should be clearly visible and offer directions in different formats or languages to support all families. Consider using illustrations or photographs in addition to the names of places in the building such as the cafeteria, library, or gym to help with more efficient wayfinding.

- **Walls, hallways, and common areas.** Areas within the school building offer additional opportunities to highlight the various experiences, backgrounds, and cultures that are represented in the school. Photographs of students, artwork and artifacts from different cultures, flags, or inspiring words of famous people of varying backgrounds should have a place in hallways and common areas like the cafeteria, library, auditorium, and multipurpose room.

"We exchange messages and find times together to connect. Our son's teacher listens and invites us to offer ideas and support."

–Cate and Dan, parents of a 6-year-old

CHAPTER 3

Communicating With Parents

How can we strengthen communication with parents?

I was excited when my daughter started kindergarten at the school in which I was teaching. Her teacher was fairly new to the school, and I had interacted with her several times as a fellow staff member. She had come to my classroom to observe during her first year at our school and asked many thoughtful questions during staff meetings. Now, in the parent role, I was eager to get to know her as my daughter's teacher.

On the first day of kindergarten, she happily greeted my daughter and me at the classroom door and allowed me to take a quick "first-day-of-kindergarten" photo or two. Then she welcomed my daughter into the classroom and wished me a good first day. Walking away from my daughter's classroom that morning, I was a little uneasy and found myself wondering how the school year would evolve. My mind was filled with so many questions. I had not been able to attend the kindergarten open house since I was simultaneously welcoming my fourth grade families during our back-to-school fair. Thus, it was comforting to get an email update at the end of my daughter's first day along with a conference reminder for the upcoming week.

Not only did the early conference reassure me that my daughter was in caring hands, it also allowed her teacher to get a good sense of how often I wanted to hear about my daughter's progress, accomplishments, and needs. Sometimes her teacher would email or write a quick note on my daughter's work. Other times, she was willing to chat with me briefly before or after school. She always found time to connect with me to answer my questions and hear my concerns. Although I was in the same building with my daughter, I still wanted to hear from and connect with her teacher, and her communication with me seemed to be tailored to my specific concerns and needs.

Just as we cultivate rewarding relationships with our students through taking the time to connect with and communicate with them, we need to do the same with their parents. Communicating effectively with parents is a crucial element in supporting student success. Whether we teach young learners who are starting preschool or kindergarten, or we teach older learners, effective communication is important to all parents and helps build and strengthen a positive and successful partnership.

Early Communication

When I was teaching third grade, our principal required all classroom teachers to call each parent before the first day of school and personally invite them to back-to-school night. I remember feeling that calling every parent was redundant since each family received a beginning-of-the-year letter in the mail as well as an automated phone call from the school with information about the event. (See the appendix, page 79, for a sample of a beginning-of-the-year letter.) It was not until I started making the first few calls that I began to realize how much more valuable it was for parents to get an invitation directly from the teacher. It made me think of the feeling that we sometimes get when we make a phone call to a business or organization and there is an actual human on the other end of the line to support us. As teachers, we have the opportunity to be that person, extending an invitation in a friendly and welcoming tone and letting parents know how valued they are—something an automated phone call could not authentically convey.

Initiating early communication with parents sends the message that connecting with them is important. Thus, we want our first connections with parents to invite collaboration, setting the tone for positive interactions throughout the year. To facilitate these connections early on, it's important to gather specific details about contact information and methods, such as:

- How will the most current parent contact information be acquired?

- What types of contact information have parents provided to the school? (Cell phone numbers, email addresses, home addresses)

- What forms of technology for communication can parents easily access? Do they have reliable internet access? Do they have a smartphone?

- How will consistent communication be maintained in situations where the student resides in more than one household?

- What forms of communication lend themselves to being consistently managed and maintained throughout the school year? (Electronic newsletters, websites, communication apps)

- What types of support need to be in place to communicate effectively with parents whose primary language is different from the primary language used at the school?

- How frequently will communication need to occur to keep parents informed?

The answers to questions such as these are key in helping to establish effective communication early in the year. Once reliable contact information has been provided by the office or acquired from class lists, and preferred forms of communication have been established, early interactions should begin with encouraging messages. Positive notes to parents at the start of the year, as well as throughout the year, let them know that we notice and appreciate their child's progress, unique qualities, and accomplishments. Parents need to hear from us when their child is doing well, not just when they are experiencing difficulties or presenting a challenge. When parents receive feedback that highlights what their child is doing well, they are more likely to reach out with questions and be open to difficult topics of discussion (Anderson 2011). And sharing positive feedback is just as valuable for us as it is for parents. It encourages us to observe and look for the strengths and talents that are in every child. It gives us the opportunity to focus on what is working and celebrate successes.

Notes highlighting strengths and accomplishments can be brief, and should contain only positive comments. They should be separate from notes containing other information, such as calling attention to challenges or areas that need improvement; these can be conveyed at another time, for instance, in a note or progress report when difficulties first arise (see Chapter 7). A positive note to parents can quickly lose its significance when coupled with other concerns: "Jane has had so much success using different multiplication strategies in math. She needs to work on completing her work in a timely manner." Though the child's strength is mentioned first, the second sentence draws attention away from the positive observation and gives the impression that the note is intended to point out that work was not completed on time.

Initiating positive communication is a key element in working to establish a constructive relationship with parents that supports the student. Therefore, beginning communication with parents early is an important step. It allows more time to be spent getting to know parents and gaining insight about their child, and helps establish a constructive relationship with parents that will best support students.

Communicate With Meaningful Consistency

I once joined the mailing list of an organization that emailed monthly newsletters with articles, tips, and support for educators, which I enjoyed reading and found very useful. But after a while I started receiving emails weekly from the organization, and then daily. There were even days when I received two or three emails. After a few months of three or more emails a week, I started to delete them without even reading. I am sure that the organization's intent was to keep their subscribers well informed. However, the overabundance of information didn't provide readers with a sufficient amount of time to read the content, process it, and use it or respond in a fitting manner.

Communication is important. Meaningful communication is essential. We want the information that we communicate to parents to be read, and we want to allow adequate time for parents to process the information and respond if necessary. Therefore, the type of communication we establish with parents should have a meaningful and agreeable flow for all parties involved. There are some types of essential communication that every parent should receive, such as information about an event, school closing, or important dates. The frequency of these types of communication is determined by when the information needs to be conveyed. For example, a monthly newsletter might be appropriate if it conveys all the content that will be covered for the month in addition to important dates and upcoming events. (See the appendix, pages 80–82, for sample newsletters.) A syllabus outlining class content and expectations might be distributed once per semester. On the other hand, we can tailor other types of communication to parents' specific needs to convey more individual information. The frequency of these types of communication will be specific to each family and to the circumstance.

Communicating With Parents		
	Information	**Formats**
General	• Schoolwide events • School closings and delays • Class content or curriculum • Class happenings and events • Upcoming projects or tests • Field trips or outings • Class celebrations • Volunteer opportunities • Items or resources needed for class • Situations that affect the whole class	• Newsletter • Email • Communication apps • Websites (class or school) • Social media
Personalized	• Student accomplishments • Student needs • Student progress • Student observations or concerns • Concerns or questions about assignments, assessments, or projects • Requests or reminders about conferences and meetings	• Phone call • Text • Email • Communication apps • Note or letter • In-person conversation • Card or postcard • Virtual meeting

As you consider how to communicate both general and personalized information, refer to the chart above to guide your planning.

Communication Challenges

In doing the important work of building relationships and establishing communication with parents, we will inevitably run into challenging situations. Communication can be difficult for any number of reasons. Busy or incompatible schedules, language barriers, previous negative encounters, or differing perceptions about school can all present obstacles to effective communication. Though establishing effective, meaningful, and consistent communication can be stressful at times, it is important to remain optimistic and persistent. Parents care about their children's success and want to be informed when there are circumstances that affect success.

While there are always unforeseen complications, there are a few proactive strategies we can employ:

- Determine parents' preferred form of communication for urgent situations and for those that are less urgent. A parent may prefer a phone call to a text or vice versa, depending on the situation or other considerations. Ask parents how they prefer to be contacted about general matters and also urgent matters, such as a missing permission slip on the day of a field trip.

- Seek out ways to help parents bridge language barriers. Consider reaching out to colleagues to learn about commonly used resources. Consult with a parent liaison or translator and explore messaging apps that allow for communication in a family's home language.

- Be clear and open in communicating information early about curriculum, grading, attendance policies, homework, and discipline procedures. Remind parents of this information proactively so they can ask questions and share concerns.

- Be mindful of how you use social media and whether parents can access posts that share your personal information, thoughts, and opinions. If social media posts are public, be cautious about posting strong opinions that might alienate some parents and have the potential to break down relationships.

A Note to First-Year Teachers

During my first year teaching at a new school, I wanted to be a super communicator. I was so eager to try out many different types of communication. My hope was to keep parents thoroughly informed about classroom experiences and events as well as their child's weekly progress in my third grade class. I set up a website to share the content and learning for the week. I created a weekly newsletter that went home in folders, featuring an overview of the learning in every subject area, volunteer opportunities, and dates to remember. I sent home a "Parent Share Gram" every month with the same four questions that allowed parents to share their thoughts and concerns about their child. I maintained a phone log and tried to call parents every month to answer questions and share their child's progress. Additionally, I sent home weekly progress reports outlining students' progress in every subject area including citizenship and homework. Now, anyone reading this might be thinking, "That is a lot." And it was. It was too much, and it was challenging to maintain for an entire class for the whole school year. Each type of communication was fine, but all together they were overwhelming. I needed to make things more manageable for me and for parents.

To help keep communication reasonable and productive for both you and parents, consider the following:

- If you are new to a school, grade level, or team, consult with colleagues to find out what types of communication are currently used and gain support and ideas about how to implement those forms of communication.

- Begin with one or two communication methods that can be easily and consistently maintained throughout the year.

- Be open to including additional forms of communication as needed as the year progresses, for an entire class or section or for specific parents.

- Create a system that works for your schedule. If your goal is to call or send personal notes or progress updates to a certain number of parents per week, choose a number that you can maintain and that doesn't feel overwhelming. (See the appendix, pages 83–86, for samples of ways to record various types of communication.)

Quick Tips

- **Respond as soon as possible.** A note, a phone call, an app notification, a text, or an email from a parent can come at any time. Conveying the message that parents' concerns, thoughts, and questions are heard is important. However, we may not always be in a position to carefully read a message and thoughtfully respond to a parent right away. Consider sending parents a quick response letting them know that you received their message and will respond more fully as soon as you are able. Then set aside time to provide a more detailed response.

- **Establish realistic boundaries.** It is important to establish realistic boundaries that support communicating with parents at reasonable times of the day. Let parents know, for example, that they can expect a response to an email or phone call within a certain time frame (say, within twenty-four hours or by the end of the school day) so that you are not giving them the impression that you are available at times of the day that do not work for your schedule. Consider morning times as well as afternoon or evening times that work well for when you might reach out to or respond to parents. Communicate these times to parents so they are aware of the best times to reach out. Be cautious about responding to parents outside of established time frames. This sends parents the message that you are available at any time.

- **Determine a schedule for communication.** Begin by reviewing your class or school schedule. Which days are busiest? Which days are more flexible? What times of day provide at least fifteen uninterrupted minutes for responding to or checking in with parents? Planning ahead will help you set up a schedule you can maintain and efficiently utilize short periods of time for emails, texts, or phone calls.

Steps Toward Partnering: Formats for Communicating With Parents

- **Communication types.** There are many ways to communicate with parents. Email, phone calls, texts, websites, social media, and communication apps provide opportunities to share information with parents. Some of these formats (such as a website or social media) are better suited for sharing general information that applies to all parents, and others (email, phone calls) are best for relaying more personal information specific to a child or parent. Keep in mind that some formats require parents to have access to an electronic device, an email address, or internet. Other forms require parents to have a smartphone or device that allows them to download an app. It is important to select the types of communication that not only work for both you and the parents, but also work to best convey the needed information.

- **Newsletters.** Printed or electronic newsletters help keep parents informed about academic content, upcoming events, volunteer opportunities, and important dates. These can be sent to parents weekly, monthly, quarterly, or each semester depending on the information that needs to be conveyed and how often the information will change. If parents have provided permission, newsletters can include photographs of the learning occurring in the classroom or, in the case of electronic newsletters, links to videos.

- **Postcards, notes, emails, and letters.** A brief message can be sent to parents in the form of a postcard, note, or letter expressing a child's progress, accomplishments, and areas of growth. Consider sending messages that share students' strengths and progress at the start of the school year in addition to areas of growth two or more times as the school year progresses.

- **Parent liaisons.** A parent liaison works to build strong and positive relationships with families and can support parents who speak different languages. They can be full-time or part-time staff members or community or parent volunteers. Parent liaisons can provide resources to families that better connect them to the happenings of the school community and proactively provide clarification when needed.

"

There is honest and professional communication and a willingness to address challenges together."

–Charles and Dana, parents of children ages 8, 12, and 14

CHAPTER 4

Partnering Through Parent-Teacher Meetings

How can we build and strengthen a partnership through parent-teacher meetings?

During a chat with my friend Jen, we found ourselves discussing memorable moments from when we were in school. She recalled one particular high school incident in which she had unexpectedly received a failing grade in an English class. Apprehensive about how her parents would respond, she shared her report card with them. Knowing their child, her parents also felt that the grade was unexpectedly low, and her father requested a meeting with her English teacher. The English teacher was quick to respond and arranged a meeting with both Jen and her father.

On the day of the meeting, the English teacher welcomed them into the class-room and invited them to sit at the table. They engaged in pleasant small talk before Jen's father articulated his concerns about the grade, and asked the teacher if she would share her system for grading her students that semester. The teacher acknowledged the concern and went on to explain the grading system to Jen and her father. She informed them that one exam in particular accounted for a larger percentage of the students' grade. When the teacher had finished her explanation, Jen waited nervously for her father to respond, uncertain of what he would say. He paused, and then asked thoughtfully, "If you were in my situation, and this were your child, how would you have wanted the teacher to have communicated with you?"

During my first few years of teaching, a question like that would have had me flustered. I conducted my parent conferences in a very structured manner. I sat on the inner part of my horseshoe table and invited parents to sit on the outside facing me. Then I explained their child's work and outlined their progress in a somewhat rehearsed way, barely leaving the opportunity for questions. I am not sure how I would have answered the question Jen's father posed. Now, however, I know that question would offer an invitation to a partnership.

It's a Partnership

Whether we use the term conference, meeting, appointment, or another term, parent-teacher meetings offer the opportunity to establish strong, collaborative partnerships with parents. They give teachers a chance to further develop a cooperative bond with parents that began with phone calls, emails, or texts about positive observations such as a student's strengths and talents. They provide a platform for parents and teachers to come together and to meet a common goal: supporting the social, emotional, and academic success of the student. In order for a partnership to thrive, both parent and teacher should play an active role in supporting student progress and success. This means that each sees the other as a valuable asset and knowledgeable resource.

In order to cultivate a genuine partnership through conferences, a relationship needs to be established early, preferably before the first conference. An early connection with parents can occur through formal schoolwide events like an open house or back-to-school fair, or other options like a welcome letter, phone call, or email. Whether formal or informal, the initial connection can become a springboard to positive and consistent communication with parents before the first parent-teacher conference. As high school educator Ben Johnson (2015) points out, "[I]f a parent doesn't already know how his or her child is performing in our classes when we schedule a conference, then we've missed valuable opportunities." Connecting early helps establish a relationship and partnership that can be strengthened during a conference. A conference should allow for a deeper conversation and the sharing of ideas about a topic or situation of which parents are already well aware. A conference should not be the first time a parent hears about failing grades or other serious concerns.

Early Parent-Teacher Conferences

For many teachers, schools or districts will require a conference or meeting that is scheduled during specific times throughout the school year. The focus for these meetings is usually student academic progress. These valuable meetings allow for parents and teachers to celebrate academic successes and discuss the academic growth of the student. An early parent-teacher conference is a meeting that occurs before the school year begins or within the first few weeks of school, so the focus is less academic and more about answering parent questions and getting to know the student from the adults who know them best. A powerful way to show parents that they matter is to hold a parent meeting before school starts or during the early weeks of school, rather than waiting until the end of the term or quarter. During these meetings, parents are provided with a greater opportunity to share and teachers are given an opportunity to build relationships and gain genuine insight about students from their parents.

After teaching first, third, and fourth grades for several years, I took on the role of teaching a fourth and fifth grade combination class. Multiage classes can create many questions and concerns for parents, and I wanted to be pro-active so that parents felt comfortable about having their child in this unique learning environment. I called families to introduce myself and mailed letters to parents over the summer welcoming them to the new school year. Then I asked to meet with parents before the school year began. I provided morning, afternoon, and evening times and gave parents options for where they would like to meet—at the school, at their homes, or at an alternate location such as a library or coffee shop.

Meeting with parents early in this way was beneficial in building a positive relationship with them and establishing a partnership. Since the school year had not yet started when I reached out to parents, the goal was to learn about the students from those who knew them best, and allow for genuine conversation with questions such as:

- "What is a goal that you have for your child this year?"

- "What are some topics/subjects that your child enjoys?"

- "What is something that would be helpful for me to know about your child in order to best support them in the classroom this year?"

- "What is an area in which you feel your child could continue to grow?"

- "What is your child's approach to or feelings about homework?"

- "How does your child navigate challenges?"

- "What strengths does your child display when working with a partner or in a group?"

- "What is an area/subject in which your child has had great success?"

- "What are your child's feelings about _____ (grade level/subject area)?"

In addition to offering a chance to know more about the child, the initial meeting provides an opportunity to share information about developmental characteristics that parents sometimes wonder about or question. An excellent resource to consult on child and adolescent development is *Yardsticks: Child and Adolescent Development Ages 4–14* by Chip Wood (2017). This resource provides great insight into child and adolescent development that is helpful to share with parents.

Be Willing to Listen First

If we truly want parents to feel that what they have to say is just as important as what we have to say, we need to share the airtime during conferences. Rather than primarily being a presentation by the teacher of the child's accomplishments, progress, and areas for growth, the meeting should encourage responses from parents throughout and allow for genuine conversation to occur. As discussed in previous chapters, a teacher who is communicating effectively has already shared information about curriculum, strengths, and areas for growth before the conference, so this meeting time can really be about partnering. Inviting parents' thoughts, questions, and concerns at the start of the conference provides the opportunity for us to hear what parents most want to know or share about their child. It also sends the message that what they have to say is important. Consider using statements like the following to invite conversation:

- "Before we begin, I want to give you the opportunity to share any thoughts, concerns, or questions you might have."

- "What questions or ideas have I created with the information I have just shared with you?"

- "These are some of the things I have noticed about your child in [subject area]. What have you noticed?"

- "What thoughts do you have about what I have shared?"

- "I would like to discuss [topics] with you today. Where would you like to begin?"

Statements and questions such as these encourage conversation and invite parents' thoughts, ideas, and questions.

Careful listening during conferences and meetings also allows for the opportunity to pause and listen before responding. This can be especially helpful when parents ask difficult questions or if they are upset. Pausing provides an opportunity to process the moment and what the parent has shared and then thoughtfully formulate a response. The response might be a statement or might include a question such as "I want to make sure that I am understanding correctly. Can you share more with me about…?" Taking time to listen, pause, and then respond also allows the conference to become more of a conversation rather than a presentation.

Meeting Throughout the Year

Parent-teacher conferences have been around for a long time, and for some parents (and some teachers) they can evoke many different emotions based on past experiences, especially if those experiences were negative. Feelings of anxiety or frustration can emerge if prior conferences were used as a way to negatively point out a child's challenges or if a teacher was using a lot of technical educational terminology without explaining it. If we use the initial meeting to set a supportive, collaborative tone, subsequent conferences or meetings can continue to carry the same collaborative tone regardless of content. Furthermore, the initial meeting can become a model of good communication, integrally involving parents in their child's education (Stevens and Tollafield 2003).

Meeting with parents throughout the year provides the opportunity for consistent and ongoing dialogue about student growth, accomplishments, and progress. It may be helpful to set up a manageable schedule or rotation that allows for meetings to occur throughout the year, such as once a month or once a quarter. Or, in the case of large classes or multiple classes or sections, consider a rotation that allows meetings to happen for a set number of classes or students every other month or each semester. Additionally, try to offer a variety of time frames to accommodate a wide range of parent schedules and needs. (See the appendix, page 86, for a communication timeline checklist.)

Each conference or meeting throughout the year may have a different focus that will help in planning the structure and determining whether the conference or meeting will include the student. All conferences and meetings should be open to those who work closely to support the child's education so that everyone is well informed and has a voice in the child's learning. This might include, but is not limited to, tutors, co-teachers, or teachers who provide specialized support for the child's learning. Involving people who are central to the child's learning in meetings throughout the year helps to sustain the collaborative tone that was established early in the year.

At the close of each conference or meeting, be specific if possible about when another meeting or conference will take place. I recall closing many conferences by letting parents know that they were welcome to reach out anytime if they would like to meet again. Although true, it was a vague invitation. Imagine if every time we wrapped up a dentist visit, instead of the receptionist asking to schedule the next appointment with the dentist, they said, "Please feel free to reach out at any time if you would like to see the dentist." If that were the case, scheduling another appointment may not make it to the top of my to-do list until there was a problem. Similarly, scheduling regular meetings with parents helps to foster a positive, collaborative partnership that works proactively to support ongoing student success, rather than waiting until a problem arises.

Quick Tips

- **Provide reminders.** Using the preferred method of communication, reach out to parents a few days prior to a scheduled conference. Notes home, emails, phone calls, or communication apps reminders are helpful ways to let parents know of an upcoming conference and give parents an opportunity to reschedule if necessary.

- **Plan for parents whose primary language is not the primary language used in the school.** Establishing a positive partnership with parents means taking the time to make sure that you are communicating in a way that all parents can understand and that they feel comfortable enough to engage in conversation. Have a translator available at conferences for parents for whom English is not their first language. Consider using translation apps to support parents who speak other languages.

- **Allow for even seating.** When conferences occur in person, select a place to sit that allows all parties to be seen as equals. Consider using a circular table or sitting next to parents rather than across from them if possible. This sends the message that the conference is an opportunity to work and think collaboratively about their child's success.

- **Honor time.** When we have multiple conferences or meetings scheduled back to back, it can sometimes be frustrating for parents when they arrive at their scheduled conference time only to have to wait for the previous conference to end. Consider allowing five minutes between conferences as a buffer. Once the conference begins, letting parents know about the time frame allotted for the conference helps all parties to honor time. This is especially helpful when parents arrive later than their scheduled time. Using statements such as the following can keep everyone mindful of time:

  - "I'm excited to have this next twenty minutes to hear about your child and share some of the things that I have noticed."

  - "We have _____ minutes to spend sharing our thoughts and ideas about _____. If we find that we need more time, we can set up another meeting on/at _____ to continue to share."

○ "I want to honor our time together today, so let's take the next _____ minutes to consider ways to . . ."

○ "I am noticing that we are coming to the end of our time together. What questions can I answer for you before we close our meeting?"

Steps Toward Partnering: Strategies for Parent-Teacher Conferences

- **Conferencing options.** Consider parents' schedules, family structures, and needs in order to select a conferencing format that will best support collaboration and communication.

  ○ *In-person conferences*—Face-to-face conferences allow for a more personal connection. We are able to take note of tone and body language during these types of meetings. In-person conferences and meetings can occur in a variety of locations, such as the classroom, a conference room, the home of the family, or an alternate convenient site. Consider preparing activities for younger siblings who may need to attend the conference along with their parents.

  ○ *Virtual conferences*—Connecting through virtual platforms has become more common. Virtual conferences allow greater flexibility for those with schedules that might be trickier to navigate or who are not able to meet in person, provided they have access to a compatible device and internet.

  ○ *Phone conferences*—Sometimes a conference over the phone is the best option for both the parent and teacher. Though the parties are not able to see one another, they are still able to communicate and share ideas.

- **Conference notes.** Keeping a record of conferences and meetings allows you to refer back to the content of the meeting later, as you follow up on action steps decided during the meeting. It's also helpful to review before your next meeting with the family. Use or create a form for recording details such as the people in attendance (parents, teachers, translators, etc.), the purpose of the meeting, thoughts and questions shared by the parent, strategies and outcomes, follow-up tasks or actions, and the date and time for the next meeting. After the meeting you can send a summary to the parents to ensure you have a shared understanding of what was discussed and what follow-up, if any, was agreed on. (See the appendix, pages 87–90, for a sample form to use to record meeting content and a sample form for a summary to share with parents.)

"With all our children, from elementary school through high school, there were always opportunities to volunteer. We were welcome and always willing to take on opportunities to help the teachers."

–Golda and Theron, parents of a 22-year-old,
a 20-year-old, and 16-year-old twins

CHAPTER 5

Strengthening Connections: Providing Engagement Opportunities

What involvement opportunities can we provide for parents?

The school in which I taught for many years was extremely diverse. It was composed of families of varying cultures from countries all over the world, and our staff spent time each year brainstorming ways we could more effectively involve parents in the life of our school community. We had made many adjustments over the years in the types of activities and events that we offered. We shifted event structures and start times based on what we knew about our families, and we worked toward creating more events and activities that were grade-level specific. We had a school PTA (parent-teacher association), but we rarely had many parents (or teachers) in attendance besides the PTA officers and school administration. During PTA meetings, events would be discussed and planned with the intention of getting more families involved, but parent involvement in these events remained uneven.

So, one year, our principal gathered together a group of staff members consisting of teachers from each grade level, an ESOL (English Speakers of Other Languages) teacher, resource teachers, specialists, and the school guidance counselor to create a committee to focus on building stronger connections with parents and gaining greater insight as to how parents would like to be involved in the classroom and school community. During the meeting, each grade-level teacher reviewed their class list and noted parents with whom they felt they had built a solid partnership. As staff members shared the names of these parents, we noticed that they were parents who were already involved in classroom or school activities in various ways throughout the school year. A question emerged: How can we learn from these parents' involvement in order to better involve all parents? This question turned out to have complex answers, and it prompted a deeper discussion about establishing more effective parent involvement opportunities in our school.

The Impact of Parent Involvement

Parent involvement is an important component in student success at every level, from elementary school to high school. The greater the involvement of parents, the greater the positive impact on student learning. Years of research attest to the positive impact of parent involvement on student success in school regardless of socioeconomic status or ethnic background (Edutopia 2000). In her article "The Eight Ps of Parent Engagement," Heather Wolpert-Gawron (2019) cites several of these benefits, including:

- Higher grades and test scores

- Better acclimation to the school environment

- Improved social skills and behavior

- Greater likelihood of continuing to higher education

Because parent involvement yields positive benefits for students, creating opportunities for parents to be involved in the classroom or school community is essential. However, we must be thoughtful and deliberate about how we involve parents in classroom and school life so that we maximize their participation and strengthen the parent-teacher relationship.

It can be tricky to establish effective involvement opportunities if we are uncomfortable with parents participating in various tasks, events, and activities in our schools or classrooms. During my first two years of teaching, I was nervous, even a little fearful, about having parents in my classroom. I was worried that a parent would question or judge the way I taught or compare me to the previous teacher. By my third year of teaching, I began to understand that parents genuinely wanted to provide support. One parent saw me after school sorting papers and offered to come in every week to do this task. Another parent had heard that we were responsible for changing the bulletin board display outside of the classroom every month and offered to help. I started to realize that not only did I need to shift my thinking about parent involvement, I also needed to be thoughtful and purposeful about the ways I involved parents in the classroom community and to see them as partners in supporting their children's success.

One of the first steps to establishing beneficial involvement opportunities for parents is to identify our own thoughts and feelings about parent involvement in the classroom and school. As mentioned in previous chapters, our beliefs and perceptions can either foster parent involvement or create barriers. We may feel that it's just one more thing added to our already overflowing plates. However, if we shift our perception, we see that effectively involving parents can serve to lessen the many tasks we have to accomplish throughout the year. We may also fear that parents will question our methods or decisions. A shift in our thinking about this can allow us to see questions as an invitation for conversation and an opportunity to provide clarity or implement needed changes. Or perhaps we feel that involving parents in the classroom conveys a lack of control. A shift in our perception here can help us to see that involving parents shows a willingness to collaborate and partner with them in the classroom.

To gain a better sense of our own mindset as we seek to involve parents more effectively in school life, reflecting on statements such as the following can help.

	Never	Rarely	Sometimes	Frequently
1. I feel anxious or bothered when I encounter parents in the school building.	◯	◯	◯	◯
2. I feel anxious or bothered when parents are in my classroom.	◯	◯	◯	◯
3. It is difficult for me to find ways for parents to assist or participate in the classroom.	◯	◯	◯	◯
4. I am bothered or flustered when parents offer ways to assist or participate in the classroom that I have not established or encountered.	◯	◯	◯	◯
5. I prefer to take care of most classroom/school tasks or activities, such as gathering resources, on my own rather than delegate them to a parent.	◯	◯	◯	◯

Just as considering our beliefs about parents is beneficial when it comes to welcoming them into our schools and classrooms, investing time in considering our thoughts and feelings about parent involvement is helpful in laying the groundwork for their participation. If we have reservations about parent involvement, we are less likely to offer them opportunities to be involved in our classrooms or schools. Therefore, it helps to be aware of any feelings and thoughts that cause us to feel uncomfortable or be hesitant so that we can take steps to shift our mindset.

Considering Involvement Opportunities

With each new year and grade level I taught, the ways in which I invited parents to get involved varied based on the needs of my students and the ways in which parents were willing to provide support in the classroom. Some years I invited parents to come in and read with students during the language arts block. Other years I invited parents to join Morning Meetings. I also invited parents to join in the learning of a new math or social studies unit for a few weeks, especially if the strategies or techniques we were using during that unit might be new or unfamiliar for parents. And still other years I asked parents to help with flyers for school and class events, monitor small groups of students during word work, or serve as chaperones on field trips.

Parent participation can take on many forms depending on levels of comfort, school and classroom needs, schedules, and the families the school community serves. Any way that parents can be involved is valuable because it connects them to the classroom and shows their students that their parents and teachers both care deeply about their education. Ideally, parent involvement also helps the teacher or the school in some way. To create mutually beneficial opportunities for parent involvement in the school community, consider these questions:

- How will parents be made aware of involvement opportunities?

- Will involvement opportunities be communicated at the start of the year in addition to other times in the year (monthly, quarterly, each semester)?

- How have you successfully involved parents in the past?

- How can parents' skills and talents be used in both short- and long-term involvement opportunities?

- What are specific tasks or activities that parents can successfully accomplish?

- What suggestions for involvement have parents offered?

- What items or resources need to be prepared beforehand in order for parents to be successful in accomplishing a task or activity?

- Will parents work with students? If so, in what capacity?

- Is training needed? If so, how will parents be trained or prepared for involvement opportunities?

- What involvement opportunities can be offered that can be done from home?

- What regulations or restrictions, if any, will affect how parents can be involved?

- How will opportunities offered during school hours be scheduled?

- What short-term opportunities can be offered? What long-term opportunities can be offered?

The questions we ask ourselves may shift or vary depending on different factors such as the time of year, the amount of knowledge we have about the families in our school, our role in the classroom or school, or involvement opportunities that have already been established. Using questions such as these as a starting point and considering the best ways to involve parents in classroom and school life helps to ensure a rewarding and successful experience for all.

Overcoming Obstacles

We know that the benefits of parent involvement are significant, but obstacles can sometimes arise that make it challenging or inconsistent. Busy schedules, work and family obligations, language barriers, or negative past experiences can keep parents from being as involved as we and they may hope to be. Some barriers are easier to overcome than others, but having an understanding of them can aid in finding solutions.

1. **Get to know which barriers are affecting parent involvement.** One simple way to get a better picture of what might be preventing parents from being involved is to ask them. Consider gathering information by using a brief involvement survey that gives parents the opportunity to rank a list of factors that would make classroom or school participation challenging, and ideas that would make involvement more accessible or feasible. The list might include items such as scheduling difficulties, child care needs, or few opportunities of interest.

2. **Make a clear plan.** Once we have a better understanding of the barriers, we can create a realistic plan with clear, measurable goals and manageable steps. For example, if several parents speak different languages, seek translation services for communication about involvement opportunities. Or if parents need child care for younger siblings, consider opportunities in which younger children can participate or determine if child care services can be provided.

3. **Be persistent.** Some plans for parent involvement will yield amazing results, while others may need a few adjustments. If a plan is not as successful as you would have wanted, pause and reflect on the areas that need adjustments. Then determine what changes need to be made before trying the plan again.

Moving From Involvement to Engagement

One year, when I was teaching fourth grade, I attended a professional development training for a district initiative involving a proposed change to the curriculum structure. I listened to the facilitators, took notes, and conversed with my team when discussion questions were posed or tasks were assigned. When presented with the option to continue the training throughout the school year within a grade-level cohort, I chose to continue. At each meeting, I listened to the facilitators, took notes, and participated in the discussion. But throughout the year I realized there was something missing. I was not truly engaged because although participants listened to facilitators and completed tasks, we were never given the opportunity to come together as a whole group to collaborate, generate new ideas, and see how all of our ideas could work together.

In an article in *Educational Leadership*, teacher Larry Ferlazzo shares that one definition of *involve* is "to enfold or envelope," which implies "doing to," while the meaning of *engage*, "to come together and interlock," suggests "doing with" (Ferlazzo 2011). Once we get parents involved in available classroom and school opportunities, we can make the shift to listening to and embedding their ideas, thoughts, and concerns in those activities and tasks in order to create more of a collaborative partnership. Parents may already be involved in school or classroom activities such as organizing student work, chaperoning events or activities, or designing flyers and bulletin boards. Moving from parent involvement to parent engagement allows parents and teachers to share responsibilities in order to support student success. Instead of simply recruiting parents for an activity or field trip, you might ask parents to be involved in the planning process for the activity or trip, specifically about what parent responsibilities could look like during the activity or trip and what information would be helpful for parents to know beforehand. Or, truly engaging parents might involve meeting with parents afterward to gain their input on adjustments or changes to consider for the next event to strengthen its success. Through collaborative discussion, parents gain some insight into the goals and objectives in the areas in which they are involved. They are able to use involvement opportunities to support student goals, and teachers listen and provide opportunities for collaboration to reach these goals. As Ferlazzo expresses, the goal of engagement is to create a partnership, and we want to strengthen connections to have parents as collaborative partners in their child's learning (Ferlazzo 2011). That partnership begins with actively involving parents.

Quick Tips

- **Think ahead.** Take time to determine how you might want to involve parents in the classroom or school community. This think time can happen independently or with a co-teacher, a grade/subject area team, or a committee. Consider the questions that were posed earlier in this chapter to help support your thinking. It's most beneficial to think of ways to involve parents before the year starts, but you can always come up with more ideas throughout the year.

- **Reach out to all parents.** All parents have something useful and valuable to contribute. It is important to provide all parents with an opportunity to be involved. Offer ways that acknowledge their strengths, skills, preferences, and talents. Suggest ways that parents can be involved from home or at school.

- **Provide a questionnaire.** Providing parents with a questionnaire allows for their interests, talents, and skills to be most accurately and effectively matched with classroom or school needs. It also provides parents with a voice as to how they would like to be involved. Reviewing samples of questionnaires can help you create your own that will best suit your classroom or school needs. Additionally, consider various ways to make the questionnaire accessible to parents—for example, mailing a paper copy, emailing, or providing a link to an online form. Once responses have been collected, take time to review them and determine the best way to match parent interests to specific needs of your classroom or school. (See the appendix, page 91, for a sample volunteer form.)

- **Make thoughtful matches.** No one wants to feel as though they are wasting their time. We want parent involvement in the classroom or school to be enjoyable and beneficial. It can be frustrating for parents (and teachers) when parents are mismatched with an involvement opportunity. This can happen, for example, when a parent with no teaching experience, or one who has not expressed any interest in working with students, is given a role like leading a reading group or guiding students through an experiment. The result would be the same if a parent who said they would most love to work with students is asked to make copies or collate papers. Use the information you've gathered about parents' interests and skills to make matches that everyone benefits from. I once had a class volunteer who kept missing her assigned days in the classroom. In talking to her about her absences, I learned that she had no desire to work with students. I realized that she preferred to make copies, collate papers, and design bulletin boards. I was able to make that adjustment so that her time was more purposeful and better suited to her skills.

- **Acknowledge all contributions.** No matter the contribution, when parents take time to help or support, be sure to acknowledge and show appreciation for all their contributions. A "thank you" can go a long way!

Steps Toward Partnering: Strategies to Provide Parent Involvement Opportunities

Parent involvement roles. Parents can take on many different roles when given opportunities to be involved in the classroom or school. It is important to clearly identify these roles in order to provide a clear picture of expectations for parents. Roles can include, but are not limited to, the following (Davis and Yang 2005):

○ *Observer*—This is a low-risk role that allows parents to experience classroom life firsthand. Parents get the opportunity to view an aspect of student learning such as a learning task, Morning Meeting, oral presentation, lesson, an author's share, science experiment, or project-based learning experience. Depending on school or district guidelines, parents may be observers in person or through a virtual platform. Be certain to determine beforehand the length of time parents will be in the classroom and clearly communicate this to parents.

○ *Participant*—Taking on the role of a participant might be a natural step for a parent who has been an observer or is comfortable in the classroom environment. In this role, parents join in on the learning or take part in the classroom activities together with students, experiencing the learning just as the students would. Just as with the observer role, it is important to determine the length of time parents will be in the classroom.

○ *Sharer*—In the sharer role, parents have the opportunity to come into the classroom to share, or show a recording of themselves as they share, about a specific topic such as a tradition, skill, talent, or career as it relates to the learning happening in the classroom. For example, I invited a parent into the classroom to share about her Greek culture. She brought in artifacts and shared information about the land and language and provided students with information that supported their background knowledge as we started our unit on ancient Greece.

○ *Helper*—The helper role provides parents with the opportunity to be involved in a variety of school-based or home-based tasks and activities. In this role, parents can assist with clerical tasks in the classroom or at home, such as sorting articles for a project or putting labels on new books. They can provide support in the classroom by monitoring small groups of students, helping with a learning task or project, or assisting in the planning of an event or celebration. With this role, it is important to be clear with directions and expectations so that parents can be successful.

● **Setting parents up for success.** We want parents to be successful when they are involved in supporting the classroom or school community. Here are a few ways to support parent success.

○ *Provide guidelines*—Provide written guidelines for parents outlining expectations for their role in the classroom. The guidelines provided should be detailed but concise, sharing expectations for the role, class routines, class rules, and privacy. Guidelines can also include goals and tips for interacting with students. Consider posting a video on a class or school website sharing the guidelines for parents to access at any time throughout the year. (See the appendix, pages 92–93, for samples of ways to communicate guidelines to parents.)

○ *Provide training*—In some instances, such as supporting students in the classroom or assisting with a schoolwide event, it may be helpful to provide training for parents. Training should include a modeling of the role and time for practice, as well as goals, guidelines, and expectations to give parents a concrete idea of what the role entails.

○ *Provide reminders*—When parents are having difficulty recalling or following through with an expectation or guideline, provide simple, helpful reminders. For example, if a parent is supporting a student with a learning task in a way that prevents the student from using a strategy to solve the problem on their own, you might say something like "Be sure to ask questions and then walk away to give the student time to think and try out a strategy independently." If a parent's involvement is creating conflict that cannot be addressed with simple reminders, consider having a private conversation with the parent or meeting with the parent to resolve the matter.

- **Ideas for parent involvement.** The chart below provides a few ideas for various types of involvement opportunities for parents. (See the appendix, pages 94–95, for examples of volunteer sign-up sheets.)

Ideas for Involvement Opportunities in the Classroom/School

- Take pictures during class or school events
- Participate in class lessons or gatherings
- Join students for lunch
- Gather resources for projects or activities
- Help set up for projects or experiments
- Present or share about a specific topic or talent
- Provide support with technology
- Do read-alouds
- Be a conversation partner for an English language learner

Ideas for Involvement Opportunities From Home

- Design flyers
- Update class/grade-level website
- Monitor or post on school or class social media platforms
- Gather resources for projects or learning units
- Cut out letters or items for projects or bulletin boards
- Explore educational sites for future use
- Staple books or packets
- Color or create classroom models for units or projects

Ideas for Involvement Opportunities for Special Events or Activities

- Serve on the PTA/PTO
- Chaperone field trips
- Run concession stands for games or events
- Set up for school events
- Clean up after school events
- Help organize class celebrations or school dances
- Run a station for a schoolwide activity such as a game night or school fair
- Assist with fundraisers
- Make costumes, design sets, etc., for productions or shows
- Coach or provide assistance with extracurricular programs or sports

"The key to a strong and positive parent and teacher partnership is a relationship built on honest communication. Both adults have to be honest about the goal . . . the success of the child is paramount."

–Faye, grandparent of a 10-year-old

CHAPTER 6

Working Toward a Common Goal: Teaching Self-Discipline

How can we collaboratively work with parents to teach self-discipline?

I was talking to a good friend and former teacher about an incident that had occurred with her eldest daughter at school. She shared that at recess, another student had hit her daughter and so her daughter had hit that student back. As she continued to share more about the situation and how it transpired, she stated, "We teach our girls if someone hits you, you hit them back." I remember feeling a little uneasy yet curious as she explained the conversation that she and her husband had with the teacher. They were against their girls starting fights, but they felt it was very important for their girls to always defend themselves. She went on to share that the teacher did not have a response.

I thought about what I had always taught my daughter: that when conflict arises, use your words. Speak. Do not stay silent. It occurred to me that my friend and I were both teaching our children assertiveness, to stand up for themselves. We were teaching the same skill but in different ways with the ultimate goal being the same—preparing our children to be assertive not just in school but out in the world.

When it comes to teaching children the skills they need to be successful both in and out of school, I learned there can be several roads to the same destination. As educators, if we are to partner with parents to meet a shared goal, we have to be open to hearing ideas that differ from our own, especially when it comes to teaching students to develop the internal controls that are needed to exhibit socially responsible behaviors. The journey to reaching a mutual understanding about teaching students self-control and socially responsible behaviors requires communication, openness, and transparency from both parents and teachers.

Teaching Self-Discipline

The word *discipline* can provoke a wide range of thoughts and feelings, both positive and negative. There are many ideas about what discipline means, many ways to think about it, and many approaches to discipline. Some feel that discipline is a system of rewards and punishments, while others view it as a way to establish order and compliance. For educators, the most effective way to support discipline is to establish a system in which students develop internal, or intrinsic, motivation, as opposed to extrinsic motivation. Thus, it is helpful if we approach this idea by thinking not about *discipline* per se, but about *teaching self-discipline*. When we consider the important role of parents and teachers in the lives of students, the most fitting approach to discipline is one that involves teaching students the skills they need to be successful in and out of school.

Teaching discipline involves providing students with clear expectations for behaviors and conduct that the teacher then enforces and reinforces to maintain order. Teaching self-discipline takes teaching discipline a step further. It means we help students become more aware of their actions and the positive and negative results of those actions so that they learn the skills they need to successfully and consistently regulate their behavior in and outside of the classroom when there are no adults present. And, because students are human and will inevitably make mistakes, we teach them the skills they need to get back on track.

With the subject area content we teach, we take the time to learn and understand the content and then consider the ways we will convey it to students so they develop a true understanding. If we know our content well, we are also familiar with aspects of the content that will likely present a challenge for students, and we are prepared to teach multiple strategies to allow students to access the content in a way that will enable them to be most successful. The same process applies to teaching self-discipline. We have to take the time to get to know our students well and build solid relationships. We have to get to know their strengths and areas in which they need greater support, and spend time building and strengthening relationships. One way to strengthen relationships with students is to gain a firm understanding of where they are developmentally and to have developmentally appropriate expectations.

When I went from teaching fourth grade to teaching first grade, I initially had a rule that during the reading block, my first graders were to read silently.

Those of you who teach younger learners are probably thinking, "That is not developmentally appropriate," and you would be correct. First graders tend to be comfortable with a busy level of noise and activity. Most often, first graders are in a stage of learning to read in which reading aloud helps them process what they are reading. Therefore, reprimanding students for being loud during the reading block was not developmentally appropriate. I had created a guideline that did not set students up for success. According to Chip Wood, author of *Yardsticks: Child and Adolescent Development Ages 4–14* (2017), when it comes to child and adolescent development, there are four key maxims that we should keep in mind:

1. Stages of growth and development follow a reasonably predictable pattern.

2. Children and adolescents do not proceed through each stage at the same pace.

3. Children and adolescents progress through the various aspects of development at their own rate.

4. Growth is uneven.

As we consider developmentally appropriate expectations and work to craft and refine our approach to teaching self-discipline, it helps to keep these maxims in mind. The more we know about our students, the stronger our relationship with them will be; and the stronger the relationship, the more teaching and learning can happen.

Initial Communication: Including Student and Parent Voice

When it comes to working toward the goal of teaching self-discipline, students play the starring role. It is important to communicate our approach to teaching self-discipline to students, and it is even more beneficial when students have a voice in the process of developing the guidelines needed to be successful in meeting expectations. When students have a clear understanding of expectations and the role they play in meeting those expectations, they are more likely to be successful. Furthermore, including students in the process of creating guidelines or rules for the classroom or school community encourages buy-in and allows us to gain a better understanding of the skills students need in order for them to successfully meet expectations (van Woerkom 2018). This increases their investment in and understanding of the purpose for the rules and the expectations that go along with them.

When we have shaped our approach to teaching self-discipline in a way that supports student success and growth, clearly communicating that approach to parents is just as important. And while there should be a shared understanding between parents and teachers of what teaching self-discipline looks like, it's important to bear in mind that discussions about this topic can be fraught because there are so many views on and approaches to it.

Some parents may believe that the teacher's approach to discipline is the only way, even if they have different opinions. Other parents will strongly disagree with our approach.

Although some of these conversations will inevitably feel less comfortable for us (and the parents) than others, it is critical that parents be encouraged to share their own thoughts, ideas, and insights. The knowledge that parents possess about their children provides valuable background information that supports us in setting and teaching realistic expectations. And whether or not our approach to self-discipline aligns with those of parents, in order to set the stage for a true collaborative partnership that endures when students do not meet expectations for behavior, it is essential to discuss our approach with parents early in the year as we are building relationships with them. In discussing our approach, it is important to share classroom guidelines and expectations as well as schoolwide policies. An early conversation can be initiated during a conference, a welcome video, an email, an introductory newsletter, or back-to-school night. A conversation with parents about teaching self-discipline should include questions about how parents support their children in learning expectations at home such as:

- "What are some of the expectations you have for your child at home?"

- "What guidelines or rules are established at home?"

- "Who establishes the guidelines or rules at home?"

- "How do you support your child in following rules?"

- "What happens when your child has difficulty meeting expectations or following rules at home?"

Asking questions such as these provides insight about how discipline is taught at home and opens up a discussion about differences in the teaching of discipline at home and at school. Communication is especially key in situations in which parents strongly disagree about how discipline is taught. When strong differences emerge, it is important to pause and truly listen. This can be difficult, and we may feel compelled to jump in and justify our approach and our reasons. But this could cause a conversation or situation to escalate. During a conversation, we can let parents know that we've heard what they've said and would like some time to further consider what was shared. This provides processing and reflection time and allows for an opportunity to seek advice from a colleague or administrator to determine how to reach some common ground and how to best plan further conversations.

Communicating with parents early helps make the approach to discipline clear from the start and opens the door to ongoing communication throughout the year. We don't want to wait until an incident has occurred before finding out that parents have very different approaches to teaching discipline than ours or that they feel that information about our approach and expectations was never conveyed. Delaying until a disciplinary situation has arisen can make a conversation much more challenging and make it more difficult to work toward a shared goal.

Finding a Common Ground to Meet a Common Goal

One day, close to the end of the school year, my daughter's kindergarten teacher came to speak with me about an incident that had occurred on the playground that day. She shared that my daughter had organized a "fight club" in which she and her classmates were to "battle" one another using various types of kicks and punches. As I mentioned at the beginning of this chapter, I had taught my daughter to use her words, so I was shocked that she would organize her classmates to fight one another.

As the teacher went on to explain the details of what had happened, my stomach was in knots. However, her conclusion to the conversation surprised me. She explained how she was planning to handle the situation and asked for my thoughts. I did not anticipate that she would want my input, and in that moment I felt that she and I had the same goal in mind: to support my daughter and help her learn from a mistake. It was about teaching.

I shared my thoughts, and together we realized that my daughter was simulating sparring, which she had been learning to do in her tae kwon do classes. My daughter had not quite made the connection that in tae kwon do the instructors were teaching specific, controlled movements and that the sparring participants wore protective gear, so attempting the same movements with her classmates wasn't safe. If her teacher had not involved me in the conversation, she would not have gained the background information I was able to provide, which helped her better understand my daughter's behavior.

When it comes to our approach to discipline, student success should be of the utmost importance, and effectively communicating with parents is a key part of that goal. The intent behind having conversations about our approach to teaching self-discipline early is to provide parents with a starting point for collaboration throughout the year. The insights and expertise that parents provide about their children is invaluable. They can provide background about situations that might be happening at home or possible reasons why a student may be displaying certain behaviors in the classroom, such as a death in the family or the birth of a new sibling. Coupled with the relationships that we've built with students and our own observations, this background information helps us identify the skills students need to make choices that will lead to the greatest success. I am reminded of an incident that occurred when one of my fourth grade students suddenly starting yelling at one of his classmates during independent reading. I had never seen this student behave in this way. When I had a conversation with his mother about the incident, she explained that his patience had been thin the past several days because he and his younger brother were now sharing a bedroom. The information she provided gave me greater insight on how to better support her son at school with managing his temper when frustrating situations occurred.

Sometimes, even with our best attempts to establish strong relationships and communicate our approach to discipline early in the year, there may still be discipline situations that are more challenging to navigate. These might involve violations of school or district codes or regulations involving bullying, weapons, or alcohol. In most cases, the approach to discipline for these types of situations is governed by school or district leaders or administration. But the same approach still holds true. We need to be sure that we are familiar with these discipline guidelines and that we communicate them early to parents and students. When parents and students are aware of the school or district's guidelines and policies, there is a stronger opportunity for collaboration if more challenging situations arise. As mentioned in previous chapters of this book, parents want their children to be successful in school, and when we communicate our approach to discipline to parents early and clearly, and invite conversation, we create a greater opportunity for collaboration in supporting student success with expectations, developing internal controls, and being socially responsible members of the community.

Quick Tips

- **Be proactive.** If you have been at a school for a while or taught a grade level or subject area for a number of years, it is likely that you are already familiar with situations in which students struggle or have a strong developmental knowledge of the students you work with. For example, perhaps you notice that it is a lot more difficult for students to be successful with expectations at the end of the school day or you are familiar with the developmental characteristics of a particular age group that might make group work challenging and cause students to struggle in meeting expectations. Being proactive and sharing this type of information with parents can provide them with a better understanding of what to expect and can allow for a more collaborative conversation to follow when students struggle.

- **Consult helpful resources.** Consider reaching out to school staff such as the guidance counselor, school psychologist, administrators, or social worker who can provide suggestions and tips as to how to best communicate the approach to discipline to parents and suggest resources and books that assist with sharing the approach.

- **Know your approach.** It can be difficult or even uncomfortable to articulate your approach to discipline to parents when you do not have a strong understanding of the approach yourself. Being familiar and comfortable with your approach to discipline is an important part of being able to effectively communicate the approach to parents. Take the time to learn about your approach to strengthen your understanding.

Steps Toward Partnering: Strategies for Meeting the Common Goal of Teaching Self-Discipline

- **Plan a conversation.** As shared in Chapter 3, communication is key in building and strengthening relationships. Therefore, planning a conversation or a meeting to discuss discipline provides the opportunity for collaboration and strengthens the parent-teacher relationship. Keep in mind that there is likely a range of emotions that may emerge when you reach out to a parent. Thus, thoughtful planning can help to put everyone at ease. Consider these steps when planning:

  - Review and reflect on the approach to teaching self-discipline that is used in your school or classroom and create a clear and concise way to articulate the approach to parents. This could be conveyed in a notice or newsletter that goes home to parents in advance and includes pictures of students modeling rules or expectations or snippets of student input in a rules creation process.

  - Early in the year, decide on a time of day and format that would be best (early morning, evening, etc.; in-person meeting, parent coffee, virtual meeting, etc.).

  - Determine which questions to pose to parents about discipline and decide when to ask those questions—during the meeting, in advance, or both.

  - Review school policies and guidelines and have copies available.

  - Establish a time to follow up with parents who may have additional questions or concerns.

- **Invite parents to see the process.** Developing guidelines with students is a powerful step in teaching self-discipline. If your classroom or school setup allows for it, consider inviting parents to witness the process either in person or remotely. This can be a very valuable experience for parents. They get the opportunity to see the students' thinking process as well as get a glimpse into the teacher's expectations. Seeing the process can also help strengthen understanding and provide a clearer picture of an approach to teaching self-discipline.

"It is reassuring when the teacher speaks honestly with us about the challenge, offers suggestions to help, and asks us about ways we might deal with challenges at home that have been effective."

–Ben and Jeraldine, parents of children ages 4, 5, 8, 10, 12, 14, and 15

CHAPTER 7

Challenging Encounters

How can we navigate challenging encounters with parents?

I had only stepped away for a moment as my daughter began working on an assignment for class, but when I returned just a few minutes later, she was crying hysterically, "Someone hacked into my account! I'm not lying. I didn't do it!" As I tried to console her, I scanned her computer screen to try to determine what had caused such a dramatic change in her disposition. One moment she was working, and the next she was in tears.

It took a solid ten minutes to calm her down enough to share what had happened. While she was in the midst of working on her assignment, her teacher had received a message that indicated that her assignment had been submitted. Her teacher immediately reached out and inquired as to why she had submitted a blank assignment. My daughter was confused and tried to explain to her teacher that she had not submitted the assignment and was still working on it. I nodded in affirmation, reminding my daughter that I had been in the room when she started working on the assignment. Then her eyes filled with tears again as she said, "Mommy, I'm not lying! I didn't turn it in. I think someone hacked into my account." She paused, and then said, "But my teacher said I was lying."

Though I calmly told my daughter not to worry and that we would figure it out, inside I was fuming. My mind was filled with thoughts and questions: I know my daughter. Does she really know my child? Why would she think she was lying? I immediately contacted the teacher to explain the situation and request a meeting. Within a few minutes, the teacher responded and agreed to a conversation in an hour. As I waited for the meeting, I planned how I would advocate for my child and convey to her teacher my strong disapproval of how she had handled the situation.

When the time of the meeting arrived, I was still upset and ready to unleash all the thoughts that I had been contemplating over the past hour to defend my daughter. But before I could begin, the teacher's opening statement altered the direction of what could have been a heated meeting, one that might have fractured the parent-teacher relationship we had been building. She began with an apology. She explained that she had accused my daughter of not telling the truth because of the assignment notification that had appeared on her end. She went on to say that after thinking about it, she realized that there could have been other reasons why the assignment came through blank. The teacher's opening put me at ease and paved the way for a meeting that focused on problem-solving and brainstorming ways to support my daughter's success with the assignment.

It is likely that at some point we will experience a challenging encounter with a parent in which emotions run high. The situation could be the result of a comment, decision, or disagreement over an academic matter; a behavior issue; a miscommunication; or a combination of these. This kind of potential conflict can produce feelings of frustration, anger, anxiety, fear, stress, or confusion for all parties involved. In the midst of it all, it can be easy to lose sight of what matters most: the student's success and our understanding of parents as valuable allies. Determining positive and effective ways to navigate tricky situations with parents is essential in establishing and maintaining positive relationships with parents for the future.

Putting It in Perspective

Challenging situations with parents can have us feeling more defensive than we would like. It is important to keep a fundamental belief in mind: all parents want what's best for their child. "The majority of parents have one basic motivation—their child is the most important thing in the world for them, and they will protect [them] at all costs, against all threats" (Mandel 2007). Parents want their child to experience academic success and develop positive relationships. They want to know that their child is being cared for in school and set up for success. Considering the parent's perspective is the first step to taking a proactive approach to navigating challenging encounters. If we want to effectively collaborate with parents when challenges arise, we need to be on the same team. Parents should view us as partners who also have their child's best interests at heart. Practicing empathy for parents and stepping into their shoes to better understand their perspective can be valuable tools for persisting through challenging events.

Taking a Proactive Approach

The benefits of establishing positive relationships with parents early in the year have been discussed throughout this book, and a foundation of trust is especially important and helpful for everyone involved in the event of a difficult discussion. When parents know that we respect them and their child, and that we appreciate their child as a unique individual, they are likely to be more open to collaborative conversations and open-minded problem-solving.

Another useful proactive step is to consider some of the most common situations that lead to potential conflicts with parents, such as misunderstandings about assignments and homework, surprises with report card grades, and behavior struggles. Here are few topics to consider that can potentially cause heightened emotions.

Assignments and Homework

When I taught first grade, I thoroughly communicated the homework procedures to families so they were clear about the homework choices that were sent home each week. I had conversations with parents when there were changes to assignments so that they could successfully support their children. Clear communication about homework and assignments gave way to positive and collaborative interactions in which the parents and I could work together to help the students navigate their work.

When I shifted to teaching fourth grade, our school made a change to the homework policy. Kindergarten through fourth grade would focus only on reading, while fifth and sixth grade homework would include all subject areas. Notification about this change went home to all families at the start of the school year. It didn't occur to me to review this new policy with parents because I assumed the communication from the school was sufficient. However, in the first quarter of the school year some parents were confused and had questions, and others were frustrated when their children appeared to have no homework. One parent told me that I should have shared this information at the start of the year because it was a new practice. He was right. That year, I found that many of the tough encounters I experienced were rooted in my failure to proactively communicate the change in the homework policy to parents. Having collaborative and open-minded conversations about homework that year was harder than I had anticipated because I had not provided parents with information that would allow them to play an equal role in supporting their child's success.

Assessments, Grades, and Report Cards

One year when I read my daughter's report card, I discovered that she had received a failing grade in one area of orchestra class. I was angry—not with my daughter, but with her orchestra teacher, because he had never indicated that there was a concern. If he had communicated the problem early on, I would have been much more open to a collaborative conversation about it. Instead, we ended up having a rather tense confrontation. Parents do not like getting surprised by a failing or low grade on their child's assessment or report card. When we wait to share signs of academic problems or unsatisfactory work with parents, it takes away the opportunity for brainstorming solutions together and supporting the student's efforts to improve.

Grades and assessments help to convey a student's understanding of content and progress in a subject area. Proactively and consistently communicating grading systems and expectations to parents and students provides all parties with shared guidelines. Furthermore, if we've taught a grade level for a number of years, we are likely familiar with content areas in which students tend to struggle to demonstrate their learning on an assessment. For example, my daughter's fourth grade teacher explained to parents at the start of the year that the students might be more challenged as they learned both fourth and fifth grade math content than previously when they were learning only grade-level math. Making parents aware of tough content that might result in a less than favorable grade on an assessment or report card sets reasonable and shared expectations.

Being prompt and consistent about communicating students' grades through-out the year invites conversation and gives parents a chance to respond and ask questions. This is especially key when a student's grades are poor or decline, if a student is not demonstrating the expected effort in class or on assignments, or if a student receives a failing grade on an assignment or assessment that counts for a large percentage of their grade. In cases such as this, it is import-ant to reach out to parents as soon as possible to discuss ways to support the student before it is too late. In some situations, it may be appropriate to include the student in the conversation. A student's input can provide additional infor-mation that can support efforts to address the situation and to determine the best way to support growth and progress. In sharing less than favorable grades with parents early or consistently, we must keep in mind that parents may still respond in an unfavorable manner. When this occurs, it is important to remain calm, listen with empathy, and consider how to collaborate with the parent to determine how to best support the student.

Academic Struggles, Retention, and Referrals for Additional Services

Academic difficulties, discussions about retention, and referrals for special services are topics that generate strong feelings. When a student is struggling and not meeting grade-level benchmarks, even when they are clearly showing effort and are receiving the teacher's support, it can be hard information for a parent to process. Early conversations with parents provide a forum for ongoing updates and allow for discussion of possible additional services and options. A friend of mine shared that it broke her heart when she realized that her daughter was struggling with reading in the third grade. However, she and her daughter's teacher had many conversations about her daughter's reading progress, so when a referral for special services was recommended, she felt prepared and at ease knowing that her daughter would be getting the support she needed.

As we deepen our relationships with students and learn more about their strengths, talents, and interests, we also gain greater insight into areas in which they struggle academically or need more support. Making parents aware of concerns as soon as we notice them invites cooperation and open dialogue if concerns or struggles persist.

Behavior Challenges

Students may struggle with meeting expectations for behavior for a variety of reasons, from frustration with assignments or classmates to adverse situations they are facing outside of school. Establishing and maintaining strong relationships with students is key when navigating challenging behaviors. When relationships are strong, we immediately notice behaviors that are out of character and are negatively impacting the child's learning or relationships. We are then able to inform parents of what we are noticing in a way that keeps parents in the loop. If we are proactive in communicating with parents in a calm and reassuring way when a counterproductive behavior arises, they will not be caught by surprise if the problem behavior persists or escalates, and they will likely be more willing to share their own insights into their child's behavior and to be a partner in problem-solving.

Responding to Challenging Encounters

Despite our best efforts to be proactive in preventing and reducing tough interactions with parents, they will still arise. When parents express feelings of frustration, anger, distress, or irritation, it can cause us to become defensive and take on an oppositional role. This can damage the relationship and hinder our efforts at collaboration. Here are a few things we can do to help ease a difficult encounter.

- **Stay calm.** It can be hard to maintain a calm demeanor when a parent is upset. However, resolving to stay calm allows us to listen and gain a better sense of the parent's true concerns and can keep a tense situation from escalating. Showing calmness may require waiting a few moments before responding to an email from a frustrated or upset parent so that our response conveys a tone of understanding rather than opposition and invites collaboration.

- **Keep the main goal in mind.** Remember that parents want the best for their child. When emotions run high, it is essential to remind ourselves of this truth and the importance of having parents as allies who possess great insight and knowledge about their child.

- **Actively listen and ask questions.** When we listen actively to a parent who is emphatically expressing a concern or who is outright upset, we must give our sincere attention to the parent and what is truly being shared. Listening actively builds our understanding so we communicate more effectively and helps us formulate questions that will clarify their concerns and reveal possible misunderstandings.

- **Provide realistic and genuine feedback.** Let parents know what you can do to support them and their child's success. Guide parents in brainstorming ways they can also provide support from home with questions such as "What have you noticed?" and "What is something that has worked well in the past?" Provide realistic timelines and solutions when addressing a problem. For example, it might be more realistic to share their child's progress weekly rather than daily. Also, be willing to let parents know if you need more time to work through a situation or if you need to get support from additional staff members such as a guidance counselor or resource teacher. Schedule times to follow up or check in as necessary.

- **Be willing to admit fault.** We're human, and therefore we make mistakes. Sometimes a stressful interaction is a result of a mistake in how we handled a situation with a student or how we approached the parents about it. We can help to diffuse a heightened situation with a parent when we acknowledge that a mistake has been made, sincerely apologize, and then work toward correcting it.

Repairing the Partnership

There may be times when a difficult situation with parents does not end with a satisfactory solution and they remain upset or frustrated. Even if a situation is resolved and tempers cool, the relationship may still remain strained. However it happens, when the partnership has been fractured it is essential to consciously work toward rebuilding it. Here are a few suggestions to aid in this process.

- **Keep parents involved.** Parents will still want to know how their child is doing in school. After a difficult encounter, it is even more important to keep parents in the loop. Send a brief note, text, or email to continue to keep them informed of progress concerning their child and make them aware of the ways you are continuing to support their child's success. This is also an opportunity to remind parents about the progress being made on any course of action that was previously agreed upon.

- **Invite parent input.** We don't have to be the ones with all the solutions. As part of your efforts to reestablish a strong relationship with parents, be sure they know that you welcome their feedback and observations of what they are noticing outside of school. When appropriate, offer to meet with them to continue the dialogue. Encouraging parent input underscores the message that parents' ideas and thoughts are valuable in the problem-solving process.

- **Consult others and use available resources.** There will be situations that are complex or thorny enough to require assistance from others. If parents remain upset, it is important to let an administrator or principal know what is happening so they can provide appropriate support. Consulting with a school guidance counselor or psychologist for additional insight, expertise, and resources can also be beneficial. They can potentially help all parties make progress with a difficult issue and work toward healing the relationship. It may also be beneficial to reach out to a teacher who has had a strong relationship with the parent in the past, as they may be able to provide additional insight.

Quick Tips

- **Pause.** It sounds so simple but can be difficult to remember when we find ourselves in the midst of a troubling situation. It can be tempting to formulate a response while a parent is speaking. Pausing provides the opportunity to think, process, and reflect, whether it's during a conversation or after an exchange has occurred. Pausing also allows us to thoughtfully consider a situation and possible outcomes, as when my daughter's fifth grade teacher realized there might be other reasons why an assignment was submitted blank. Pausing is a powerful way to work toward a more productive conversation with a parent.

- **Respond with understanding.** In a conversation with a parent, the way we respond can make a huge difference in the outcome. After a parent has shared thoughts, summarize and ask questions to be sure you understand. Make sure your responses convey understanding as well as support. Use language such as:

  - "I can tell that this is really important to you."

  - "I want to make sure that I understand what you just shared with me. Is it that . . . ?"

Steps Toward Partnering: Strategies to Navigate Challenging Encounters With Parents

- **Set the tone.** Challenging encounters are tough, so we want to set a positive tone that puts parents at ease. This means creating a welcoming climate of understanding and empathy. Setting the tone begins by doing a self-check. Our tone and body language convey a lot. Check your body positioning and your facial expression. Are they inviting and open? Is your nonverbal communication inviting collaboration? Your first words to begin a conversation in all difficult situations should invite productive conversation. State the goal and thank parents for taking the time to talk and work through the situation with you. For example, you might say, "I appreciate you taking the time to talk with me today so we can work together to determine the best way to support Jane." Share concerns in a calm and assuring way, such as "It seems as though Jane has had a rough couple of days. She's had a tough time working cooperatively with her group and did not complete her writing. We were able to talk and think through how to express her thoughts and ideas in a productive way. I feel confident that she'll be successful in the upcoming days, but I just wanted to let you know so that we can keep an eye on this. Is there anything you feel we can do to further encourage and support her?"

- **Use language that conveys empathy.** Empathetic language can go a long way toward reducing tension and enhancing open communication during a difficult encounter with parents. The following sentences and sentence starters are examples of how to show empathy and communicate your positive intentions:

  - "It sounds like you are really thinking about what might best support your child. Here are some ways I can help . . ."

  - "I want to be sure that I am able to provide you with as much support as I am able. Let me check with _____ and get back to you on ____. In the meantime, I will plan to . . ."

  - "I would be happy to discuss this further. Allow me to get back to you tomorrow with a few possible days and times for us to meet."

  - "Can you share more about . . . ?"

  - "What is something that has worked for your child that you would be willing to share with me?"

  - "I'm sure _____ [situation] can be _____ [difficult, sad, stressful, etc.]. How can I help your child while they are at school?"

  - "I appreciate your bringing this to my attention."

- **Collect and provide supporting documentation.** Sometimes, providing supporting documentation in conjunction with a concern can help parents gain a better understanding of an issue and clear up any misunderstandings. When problems arise, take time to observe and keep documentation on the issue. This can be in the form of work samples, anecdotal records, assessment results, behavior records, and notes from previous meetings or conferences. Provide supporting documentation to aid in problem-solving and collaboration rather than using it in what might be construed as a counterattack.

AFTERWORD

As I wrapped up the work on this book, my daughter started middle school. It wasn't just the newness of the next phase in her education that filled me with a mixture of excitement and nervousness; it was also a new school, in a new city, in a new district, with eight new teachers. That is a lot of new, and I found myself wondering how the relationship with each teacher would form and develop. After a week of school, I received an introductory email from one of the teachers. And although the same email template may have been used for every parent, I remember how I felt when I received it. I felt welcomed.

As educators, with each new school year, each new semester, and each new class we get the opportunity to set goals for, grow, reflect on, and refine connections with parents. Those first seeds of connection that we plant are so essential and need to be nurtured. With much care and diligence, we can cultivate relationships with parents that grow into wonderful partnerships.

I used to think it was good enough to establish strong relationships with a few parents. Over the years, and in the writing of this book, I have learned that establishing strong relationships with all parents is tough work, but it is absolutely worth it because they help to support the most important goal of all: the success of each and every one of our students.

Beginning-of-the-Year Letter

Welcome to Ms. Cofie's Class

I am excited to have your child in my class, and I'm looking forward to a spectacular year!

I want your child to have a successful school year. Part of making this year a success is ensuring that your child will have a safe and caring environment in which to learn. In order to accomplish this goal, the first several weeks of school will be used to help students become familiar with the procedures they will need to know and follow throughout the school year. These include various procedures such as learning the morning routine, properly using classroom supplies, and completing assignments. We will practice and review the procedures until they have become familiar and revisit them throughout the school year as needed.

I hope to see you at back-to-school night on Thursday, September 21, at 7:00 pm so that I can share all the exciting things your child will be learning this year. You will also have the opportunity to schedule a parent-teacher conference so we can discuss your goals for your child.

I look forward to working with you to make this a successful school year for your child!

Sincerely,

Jane Cofie

Sample Newsletters

News From Room 13

Tuesday, January 7 • Number 4

Language Arts

We are quite the readers in third grade! During reading workshop we have been studying various folktales and setting our purpose for reading. We've been reading to make, confirm, and revise predictions; make connections; and organize events logically. We will continue to think about our reading this month as we learn to summarize and understand basic plots of various fiction genres.

As your child reads at home, have them make predictions about the text and sequence the major events. This will help strengthen comprehension. Remember that students should be reading every night for 20 minutes or more and setting the purpose for reading on their reading bingo blackout sheet. Please have your child retell and share the story with you before signing the bingo sheet each night.

We have been studying various word patterns and have been learning activities to help strengthen our study of words. Next month, students will be bringing home word study contracts. The contracts will contain words and activities learned at school that the students will complete at home. The activities for next month include: spelling sentences, rainbow words, cursive words, word find, spelling illustrations, bubble words, karate words, opera words, and sign language words. Word study contracts will be due on Mondays unless otherwise stated.

During writing workshop we have been working hard on our writing. We have been paying particularly close attention to the process of writing, and we are learning to use the process to compose personal narratives, nonfiction, and fiction pieces.

Math

We have really been busy in math! Lately we have been focusing on solving problems that involve sums and differences of numbers less than 9,999. Subtraction across zeros has been rather tricky, but we are working hard to understand the concept of regrouping so we will be ready to add and subtract decimals, fractions, and money later in the month of January. Your child should expect to be assessed on concepts involving adding and subtracting decimals and fractions on Friday, January 11. Be sure to check your child's assignment book for updates!

Social Studies

We are quite the economics experts and are now ready to tackle ancient civilizations, beginning with Greece. We will study the physical and human characteristics, adaptations, and contributions of the ancient Greek civilization. Your child should expect to be assessed by the end of the month. Be sure to review your child's social studies interactive notebook to see what we've been studying!

During this month your child is responsible for completing a civilization project which is due on January 18. The information about this project went home before the winter break. We will share the projects in class later this month.

Science

We have been studying energy from the sun and various Earth cycles that include the sun, such as day and night, seasons, phases of the moon, and the tides. We will wrap up our study of Earth cycles with the water cycle.

Be on the lookout for a great place to see the moon! During our study of the moon phases, your child has been asked to observe the moon each night and draw the phase observed. Be sure to check out your child's interactive notebook every Tuesday night this month to see what exciting Earth cycles we have been studying!

What's New!

Would you like a way to build your child's library at home? Scholastic offers a selection of many great books. If you are interested in ordering for your child, visit www.scholastic.com and use our unique class code!

VOLUNTEER OPPORTUNITIES

Would you like to be a part of our Morning Meetings? Join us on Friday mornings from 9:15 to 9:45. Please call to R.S.V.P.

We are in need of donations of glue sticks.

Dates to Remember

January 18 – Civilization Project Due

January 21 – Holiday

January 24 – Family Science Night

January 24 – 2nd Grading Period Ends

January 25 – Student Holiday

January 28 – Student Holiday

What's the News?

Week of
DECEMBER 14

We have been learning so much and growing as a classroom community! These past weeks have challenged us to discover ways to support one another and the guests who visit our room. We've been encouraging one another to persevere with challenging learning tasks, and we have been supporting and celebrating one another's successes. We can't wait to see what the New Year will bring!

During the break, take time to relax and enjoy time with family and friends. Have a wonderful and very safe winter break, and I'll see you in the New Year!

This week we . . .

- **Reading** – worked on formulating questions from headings in nonfiction
- **Writing** – revised and edited our personal narratives
- **Math** – focused on creating equivalencies with rational numbers
- **Science** – learned about our solar system's planets
- **Social Studies** – learned about why the Jamestown settlers came
- **Health** – started our unit on nutrition

When we return in the New Year, we will . . .

- **Reading** – focus on main idea and supporting details in nonfiction
- **Writing** – begin prewriting techniques for fiction writing
- **Math** – continue with rational numbers
- **Science** – continue studying our solar system and looking at the moon phases
- **Social Studies** – discover the hardships encountered in Jamestown
- **Health** – continue our unit on nutrition

UPCOMING EVENTS:
December 21–January 1 – winter break
January 7 – PTA Health and Fitness Night

Communication Records

Communication Frequency Record Sheet

Grade Level/Class: _____

Month/Quarter/Semester: _____

Student Name	Type of Communication									
	Note		Email		Text		Phone Call		Meeting	
Jamie L.	9/8		9/28				9/14			
Quincy M.	9/8		9/15	9/16			9/14			
Arya P.	9/8						9/14		9/28	

Individual Student Phone Log

Student Name: __Trinity O__   Phone Number: _____

Date	Time	Spoke to	Reason for Call	Outcome
9/7	11:50	Grandma (Thelma)	Invitation to back-to-school night on September 21	Her daughter will attend but will need to leave a few minutes early.
9/27	4:05	Dad (Mr. O)	Reminder about tomorrow's welcome conference at 8:00 a.m.	Both he and his wife will be there.

Class Phone Log

Month: __September__   Class: __History 1__

Student	Phone Number	Date	Time	Spoke to	Reason for Call	Outcome
Trinity O	713-555-5555	9/7	11:50	Grandma (Thelma)	Invitation to back-to-school night on September 21	Her daughter will attend but will need to leave a few minutes early.
Joseph S	713-555-6543	9/7	11:55	Joann	Invitation to back-to-school night on September 21	She will be attending

Communication Timeline Checklist

Grade Level/Class: _____

August/September
Welcome phone call, text, email, letter, video, etc.
Beginning-of-the-year welcome event (back-to-school night, open house, etc.)
Schedule parent conferences
Send student strength and success notes, emails, calls, texts, etc.
Parent-teacher conferences
First newsletter/website or social media introduction
Share parent volunteer opportunities
Other:

October/November
Parent-teacher conferences
Communicate student progress and areas of growth
Second newsletter/update website or social media
Send student strength and success notes, emails, calls, texts, etc.
Schedule possible check-in meetings
Guide and support parent volunteers
Other:

December/January
Communicate student progress and areas of growth
Third newsletter/update website or social media
Send student strength and success notes, emails, calls, texts, etc.
Schedule possible check-in meetings
Guide and support parent volunteers
Other:

February/March
Communicate student progress and areas of growth
Fourth newsletter/update website or social media
Send student strength and success notes, emails, calls, texts, etc.
Schedule possible check-in meetings
Other:

April/May/June
Final parent-teacher conferences
Communicate overall student progress for the year
Final newsletter, website, or social media updates
Send student strength and success notes, emails, calls, texts, etc.
Year-end letters or emails
Thank you notes/cards to parent volunteers
Other:

Conference Follow-Up Forms

Following up . . .

Dear Family:

Below I have summarized some of the information we discussed at our meeting. Please take a moment to review this summary, and return the bottom portion.

_____

_____

_____

_____

_____

_____

Sincerely,
Ms. Cofie

. . . .

Student name _____

○ I have reviewed the summary and do not have any questions.

○ I have reviewed the summary and have questions. Please contact me at

_____.

○ I have reviewed the summary and would like to schedule another conference.

Parent signature _____ Date _____

Student name: _____ Date: _____ Time: _____

Goals	
Academic:	Social:

Strengths/Interests:

Areas of focus:

Family concerns or questions:

Follow-up meeting/Action items:

Contact Information

Parent names: _____ _____

Home number: _____ Cell number: _____

Email: _____

Best form of contact   email   cell   note home   home phone

Student name: _____ Date: _____ Time: _____

Grade level/Subject area: _____

People present: _____

_____

Conference focus:

Teacher action plan:

Family/Student action plan:

Follow-up:

Next meeting:

Student name: _____ Date: _____ Time: _____

Grade level/Subject area: _____

Attendees: _____

_____

Purpose: _____

Strengths/Successes: _____

_____

_____

_____

_____

Progress/Areas of growth: _____

_____

_____

_____

Next steps: _____

_____

_____

_____

Follow up on (task/topic): _____

_____

_____

By (date): _____

Volunteering Materials

VOLUNTEER FORM

Name _____

Child's name _____

Email address _____

Phone number _____ cell   home   work

I can help with volunteer opportunities (select one):

○ at school

○ from home

○ at school or from home

I am interested in volunteering for the following types of activities
(select all that apply):

○ donating supplies

○ making copies

○ organizing books

○ collecting resources for projects

○ posting work on or designing bulletin boards

○ chaperoning field trips

○ cutting/sorting items

○ sharing/presenting on content-related topics

○ supporting with class celebrations

○ supporting with the class newsletter/website

○ other: _____

[Date]

Dear Parents,

The children and I welcome you to visit our classroom throughout the year. Whether you come to observe, share something, take part in classroom activities, or help out, we look forward to having you.

Our goal in this classroom is for students to be independent workers who support one another by working cooperatively and with self-control. To encourage this, and to help ensure that your visit is a positive experience for everyone, please keep these tips in mind:

- During independent work times, feel free to interact with students by asking them to tell you about their work or what they're doing.

- If you're observing a lesson, focus on what the students are doing. If you have any questions to ask me, please save them until after I've finished working with the students.

- Interact with other students in addition to your own child.

- Give help only when a student asks for it, and start by asking the student what they have already tried.

- Please follow the rules of our classroom, particularly the signals we use. The chime sound or a raised hand means "Freeze. Quiet. Listen."

Thank you very much!

Sincerely,
[Teacher's name]

(From *Parents and Teachers Working Together* by Carol Davis and Alice Yang)

CLASSROOM VOLUNTEER GUIDELINES

Welcome to our classroom! We are happy to have you with us today. Please review the guidelines below to help make your visit today a success.

- Be sure to model and follow our rules and signals for attention.

- When working with students or observing student learning, allow for productive struggle. This means providing help only when a student asks and using prompts such as:

    - *Tell me what you have tried.*

    - *What is a strategy you could try?*

    - *What information do you already know?*

    - *What is a helpful strategy or solution that someone else in your class might suggest?*

    - *How can I help you work through this?*

    - *How have you solved similar problems?*

- Keep the learning going. Whether you are observing, helping in the background, or supporting students and their work, the goal is to always allow students to do their best thinking and learning.

VOLUNTEER!

Would you like to volunteer? Sign up below.

Name	Phone Number	Email Address	I would like to volunteer . . . (Circle your preference.)		
			in the school	from home	both home and school
			in the school	from home	both home and school
			in the school	from home	both home and school
			in the school	from home	both home and school
			in the school	from home	both home and school
			in the school	from home	both home and school
			in the school	from home	both home and school
			in the school	from home	both home and school
			in the school	from home	both home and school
			in the school	from home	both home and school
			in the school	from home	both home and school

FIELD TRIPS

Be a chaperone on one of our
class field trip experiences!

1. _____

2. _____

3. _____

4. _____

5. _____

SUPPLIES

Help out our class by collecting or
purchasing supplies for activities.

1. _____

2. _____

3. _____

4. _____

5. _____

CLASS CELEBRATIONS

Assist with class celebrations.

1. _____

2. _____

3. _____

4. _____

FAMILY GATHERING

Assist with our grade-level family night.

1. _____

2. _____

3. _____

4. _____

PTA REPRESENTATIVE

Represent our class at PTA meetings,
which are held once a month.

1. _____

2. _____

REFERENCES

Anderson, Mike. 2011. *What Every 3rd Grade Teacher Needs to Know.* Turners Falls, MA: Center for Responsive Schools.

Bell, Kenton, ed. 2013. *Open Education Sociology Dictionary.* https://sociology dictionary.org/.

Burnham, Kristin. 2020. *5 Culturally Responsive Teaching Strategies.* Northeastern University Graduate Programs. https://www.northeastern.edu/graduate.

Comer, James P., and Norris M. Haynes. 1991. "Parent Involvement in Schools: An Ecological Approach." *The Elementary School Journal* 90, no. 3, 271–77.

Davis, Carol, and Alice Yang. 2005. *Parents & Teachers Working Together.* Turners Falls, MA: Center for Responsive Schools.

Dee, Thomas, and Seth Gershenson. 2017. Unconscious Bias in the Classroom: Evidence and Opportunities, *Google's Computer Science Education Research.* https://goo.gl/O6Btqi.

Edutopia. 2000. "Parental Involvement Reaps Big Benefits." https://www.edutopia.org/parent-involvement-reaps-big-benefits.

Epstein, Joyce L., and Karen Clark Salinas. May 2004. "Partnering with Families and Communities." *Educational Leadership* 61, no. 8 (May): 12–18. http://citeseerx.ist.psu.edu/viewdoc/download?doi=10.1.1.494.2020&rep =rep1&type=pdf.

Ferlazzo, Larry. May 2011. "Involvement or Engagement?" *Educational Leadership* 68, no. 8 (May): 10–14.

Hammond, Zaretta. 2013. "Cultural Responsiveness Starts with Real Caring." Learning for Justice. https://www.learningforjustice.org/magazine/cultural-responsiveness-starts-with-real-caring.

Hammond, Zaretta. 2015. "3 Tips to Make Any Lesson More Culturally Responsive." Cult of Pedagogy. https://www.cultofpedagogy.com/culturally-responsive-teaching-strategies/.

Henderson, Anne T., and Karen L. Mapp. 2002. *A New Wave of Evidence: The Impact of School, Family, and Community Connections on Student Achievement*. National Center for Family and Community Connections with Schools, Southwest Educational Development Laboratory. https://sedl.org/connections/resources/evidence.pdf.

Hoover-Dempsey, Kathleen, and Joan M. T. Walker. 2002. *Family-School Communication*. Vanderbilt University. https://citeseerx.ist.psu.edu/viewdoc/download?doi=10.1.1.467.3740&rep=rep1&type=pdf.

International Federation of Library Associations and Institutions (IFLA). n.d. "Defining 'Multiculturalism.'" https://www.ifla.org/publications/defining-multiculturalism.

Johnson, Ben. 2015. "Two Kinds of Parent-Teacher Conferences." Edutopia. https://www.edutopia.org/blog/two-kinds-parent-teacher-conferences-ben-johnson.

Ladson-Billings, Gloria. 1994. *The Dreamkeepers*. San Francisco: Jossey-Bass.

Mandel, Scott. 2007. *The Parent-Teacher Partnership: How to Work Together for Student Achievement*. Chicago: Zephyr.

Stevens, Brenda A., and Andrew Tollafield. 2003. "Creating Comfortable and Productive Parent/Teacher Conferences." *Phi Delta Kappan* 84, no. 7 (March): 521–24.

Van Woerkom, Marieke. 2018. "A Proactive Approach to Discipline." Edutopia. https://www.edutopia.org/article/proactive-approach-discipline.

Wolpert-Gawron, Heather. 2019. "The Eight Ps of Parent Engagement." National Education Association. https://www.nea.org/advocating-for-change/new-from-nea/eight-ps-parent-engagement.

Wood, Chip. 2017. *Yardsticks: Child and Adolescent Development Ages 4–14*. 4th ed. Turners Falls, MA: Center for Responsive Schools.

FURTHER RESOURCES

All of the recommended practices in this book come from or are consistent with the *Responsive Classroom* approach to teaching—an evidence-based education approach associated with greater teacher effectiveness, higher student achievement, and improved school climate. *Responsive Classroom* practices help educators build competencies in four interrelated domains: engaging academics, positive community, effective management, and developmentally responsive teaching.

To learn more, see the following resources published by Center for Responsive Schools and available at www.responsiveclassroom.org.

Child Development: Understand children's common physical, social-emotional, cognitive, and language characteristics at each age, and adapt teaching to respond to children's developmental needs.

Yardsticks: Child and Adolescent Development Ages 4–14, 4th ed., by Chip Wood. 2017.

Yardsticks Guide Series: Common Developmental Characteristics in the Classroom and at Home, Grades K–8 (based on *Yardsticks* by Chip Wood). From *Responsive Classroom*. 2018.

Classroom Management: Set up and run a classroom in ways that enable the best possible teaching and learning.

Building an Academic Community: The Middle School Teacher's Guide to the First Four Weeks of the School Year. From *Responsive Classroom* with Ellie Cornecelli and Amber Searles. 2018.

Empowering Educators: A Comprehensive Guide to Teaching Grades K, 1, 2 by Kirsten Lee Howard, Amy Wade, Becky Wanless, and Lisa Dewey Wells. 2021.

Empowering Educators: A Comprehensive Guide to Teaching Grades 3, 4, 5 by Julie Kelly, Andy Moral, Jenni Lee Groegler Pierson, and Amanda Stessen-Blevins. 2021.

Empowering Educators: A Comprehensive Guide to Teaching Grades 6, 7, 8 by Linda Berger, Emily Parrelli, Brian Smith, and Heather Young. 2021.

The First Six Weeks of School, 2nd ed. From *Responsive Classroom*. 2015.

Interactive Modeling: A Powerful Technique for Teaching Children by Margaret Berry Wilson. 2012.

Teaching Children to Care: Classroom Management for Ethical and Academic Growth K–8, revised ed., by Ruth Sidney Charney. 2002.

What Every Teacher Needs to Know, K–5 series, by Margaret Berry Wilson and Mike Anderson. 2010–2011. (Includes one book at each grade level.)

Engaging Academics: Learn tools for effective teaching and making lessons lively, appropriately challenging, and purposeful to help children develop higher levels of motivation, persistence, and mastery of skills and content.

The Joyful Classroom: Practical Ways to Engage and Challenge Students K–6. From *Responsive Classroom* with Lynn Bechtel and Kristen Vincent. 2016.

The Language of Learning: Teaching Students Core Thinking, Speaking, and Listening Skills by Margaret Berry Wilson. 2014.

Make Learning Meaningful: How to Leverage the Brain's Natural Learning Cycle in K–8 Classrooms by Kristen Vincent. 2021.

Middle School Motivators: 22 Interactive Learning Structures. From *Responsive Classroom*. 2016.

Morning Meeting and Responsive Advisory Meeting: Gather as a whole class to greet each other, share news, and warm up for the day of learning ahead.

80 Morning Meeting Ideas for Grades K–2 by Susan Lattanzi Roser. 2012.

80 Morning Meeting Ideas for Grades 3–6 by Carol Davis. 2012.

150+ Purposeful Plans for Middle School. From *Responsive Classroom* with Michelle Benson, Rio Clemente, Nicole Doner, Jeannie Holenko, Dana Januszka, and Amber Searles. 2018.

Doing Language Arts in Morning Meeting: 150 Quick Activities That Connect to Your Curriculum by Jodie Luongo, Joan Riordan, and Kate Umstatter. 2015. (Includes a Common Core State Standards correlation guide.)

Doing Math in Morning Meeting: 150 Quick Activities That Connect to Your Curriculum by Andy Dousis and Margaret Berry Wilson. 2010. (Includes a Common Core State Standards correlation guide.)

Doing Science in Morning Meeting: 150 Quick Activities That Connect to Your Curriculum by Lara Webb and Margaret Berry Wilson. 2013. (Includes correlation guides to the Next Generation Science Standards and A Framework for K–12 Science Education, the basis for the standards.)

Doing Social Studies in Morning Meeting: 150 Quick Activities That Connect to Your Curriculum by Leah Carson and Jane Cofie. May 2017. (Includes correlation guides to the National Curriculum Standards for Social Studies—The Themes of Social Studies, the *College, Career, & Civic Life C3 Framework for Social Studies State Standards*, and the Common Core State Standards for English Language Arts.)

The Morning Meeting Book, 4th ed., by Karen Poplawski. 2023.

Movement, Games, Songs, and Chants: Sprinkle quick, lively activities throughout the school day to keep students energized, engaged, and alert.

50 More Energizers! Purposeful Play That Leads to Learning by Melissa Shoup Gheen. 2022.

99 Activities and Greetings: Great for Morning Meeting . . . and Other Meetings, Too! by Melissa Correa-Connolly. 2004.

Closing Circles: 50 Activities for Ending the Day in a Positive Way by Dana Januszka and Kristen Vincent. 2012.

Energizers! 88 Quick Movement Activities That Refresh and Refocus by Susan Lattanzi Roser. 2009.

Refocus and Recharge: 50 Brain Breaks for Middle Schoolers. From *Responsive Classroom*. 2016.

Positive Teacher Language: Use words and tone as a tool to promote children's active learning, sense of community, and self-discipline.

The Power of Our Words: Teacher Language That Helps Children Learn, 2nd ed., by Paula Denton, EdD. 2014.

The Power of Our Words for Middle School: Teacher Language That Helps Students Learn. From *Responsive Classroom*. 2016.

Preventing Bullying at School: Use practical strategies throughout the day to create a safe, kind environment in which bullying is far less likely to take root.

How to Bullyproof Your Classroom, 2nd ed., by Caltha Crowe. 2021. (Includes bullying prevention lessons.)

Professional Development/Staff Meetings: Learn easy-to-use structures for getting the most out of your work with colleagues.

Energize Your Meetings! 35 Interactive Learning Structures for Educators. From *Responsive Classroom.* 2014.

The Responsive Classroom Assessment Tool for Elementary Teachers, 2nd ed. From *Responsive Classroom.* 2016.

The Responsive Classroom Assessment Tool for Middle School Teachers. From *Responsive Classroom.* 2020.

Solving Behavior Problems With Children: Engage children in solving their behavior problems so they feel safe, challenged, and invested in changing.

Sammy and His Behavior Problems: Stories and Strategies from a Teacher's Year by Caltha Crowe. 2010.

Solving Thorny Behavior Problems: How Teachers and Students Can Work Together by Caltha Crowe. 2009.

Teasing, Tattling, Defiance and More: Positive Approaches to 10 Common Classroom Behaviors by Margaret Berry Wilson. 2013.

Special Area Educators: Explore key *Responsive Classroom* practices adapted for a wide variety of special areas.

Responsive Classroom for Music, Art, PE and Other Special Areas. From *Responsive Classroom.* 2016.

Teaching Discipline: Use practical strategies, such as rule creation and positive responses to misbehavior, to promote self-discipline in students and build a safe, calm, and respectful school climate.

Responsive School Discipline: Essentials for Elementary School Leaders by Chip Wood and Babs Freeman-Loftis. 2011.

Rules in School: Teaching Discipline in the Responsive Classroom, 2nd ed., by Kathryn Brady, Mary Beth Forton, and Deborah Porter. 2011.

Seeing the Good in Students: A Guide to Classroom Discipline in Middle School. From *Responsive Classroom* with Rashid Abdus-Salaam, Andy Moral, and Kathleen Wylie. 2019.

Teaching Self-Discipline: The Responsive Classroom Guide to Helping Students Dream, Behave, and Achieve in Elementary School. From *Responsive Classroom* with Laurie Badge, Suzy Ghosh, Earl Hunter II, Caitie Meehan, and Cory Wade. 2018.

About the Author

Jane Cofie began her journey as a preschool teacher over twenty years ago and since then has taught pre-K through fifth grade in Fairfax County, Virginia. She started using the *Responsive Classroom* approach with her students twelve years ago and experienced how the approach strengthened her teaching and supported her students' learning. She later became a consulting teacher and is currently the director of curriculum and instructional design for Center for Responsive Schools. When Jane is not supporting teachers or working with students, you can find her spending time with her family or playing games and watching movies with her daughter, Sierra Rose.

About the Publisher

Center for Responsive Schools, Inc., a not-for-profit educational organization, offers professional development, curriculum, and books and resources to support academic, social, and emotional learning.

Center for Responsive Schools (CRS) is the developer of *Responsive Classroom*®, a research-based education approach associated with greater teacher effectiveness, higher student achievement, and improved school climate, and of Fly Five, a comprehensive social-emotional learning curriculum for kindergarten through eighth grade.

Center for Responsive Schools' vision is to influence and inspire a world-class education for every student in every school, every day, and to bring hope and joy to educators and students alike. Visit us at crslearn.org to learn more: